W9-DGP-627

SATAN, YOU CAN'T HAVE MY MARRIAGE

IRIS DELGADO

CHARISMA
HOUSE

Most CHARISMA HOUSE BOOK GROUP products are available at special quantity discounts for bulk purchase for sales promotions, premiums, fundraising, and educational needs. For details, write Charisma House Book Group, 600 Rinehart Road, Lake Mary, Florida 32746, or telephone (407) 333-0600.

SATAN, YOU CAN'T HAVE MY MARRIAGE by Iris Delgado
Published by Charisma House
Charisma Media/Charisma House Book Group
600 Rinehart Road
Lake Mary, Florida 32746
www.charismahouse.com

Unless otherwise noted, all Scripture quotations are from the New King James Version of the Bible. Copyright © 1979, 1980, 1982 by Thomas Nelson, Inc., publishers. Used by permission.

Scripture quotations marked AMP are from the Amplified Bible. Old Testament copyright © 1965, 1987 by the Zondervan Corporation. The Amplified New Testament copyright © 1954, 1958, 1987 by the Lockman Foundation. Used by permission.

Scripture quotations marked KJV are from the King James Version of the Bible.

Scripture quotations marked NAS are from the New American Standard Bible, copyright © 1960, 1962, 1963, 1968, 1971, 1972, 1973, 1975, 1977, 1995 by The Lockman Foundation. Used by permission. (www.Lockman.org)

Scripture quotations marked NIV are from the Holy Bible, New International Version. Copyright © 1973, 1978, 1984, International Bible Society. Used by permission.

Scripture quotations marked NLT are from the Holy Bible, New Living Translation, copyright © 1996, 2004, 2007. Used by permission of Tyndale House Publishers, Inc., Wheaton, IL 60189. All rights reserved.

Scripture quotations marked THE MESSAGE are from *The Message: The Bible in Contemporary English*, copyright © 1993, 1994, 1995, 1996, 2000, 2001, 2002. Used by permission of NavPress Publishing Group.

Cover design by Justin Evans
Design Director: Bill Johnson

Visit the author's website at www.crownedwithpurpose.com.

Library of Congress Cataloging-in-Publication Data
Delgado, Iris.
  Satan, you can't have my marriage / Iris Delgado.
       p. cm.
  Includes bibliographical references (p.   ).
  ISBN 978-1-61638-673-3 (trade paper) -- ISBN 978-1-61638-674-0
(e-book) 1. Marriage--Religious aspects--Christianity. 2.
Spouses--Religious life. 3. Spiritual warfare. I. Title.
  BV4596.M3D45 2012
  248.8'44--dc23

                               2011038961

People and names in this book are composites created by the author from
her experiences as a counselor. Names and details of their stories have been
changed, and any similarity between the names and stories of individuals
described in this book to individuals known to readers is purely coincidental.

While the author has made every effort to provide accurate Internet addresses
at the time of publication, neither the publisher nor the author assumes any
responsibility for errors or for changes that occur after publication.

First Edition

12 13 14 15 16 — 987654321
Printed in the United States of America

I dedicate this book to my wonderful husband, John,
who has always displayed all the attributes of a loving and
caring husband. His total confidence in me has lifted me above the
mediocre, status quo wife into one who is eager to excel and give back an
unconditional love that is satisfying and uncompromised. His
dependence on God has affected our entire family. Thank
you for forty-one years of love, respect, and honor.

CONTENTS

FOREWORD

W HAT A DELIGHT to write this foreword. I've never met a person quite like Iris Delgado. She is not only a special friend and companion, but she is also a godly example of God's faithful love and endurance.

I have seen the quality of her character close up. During the storms of life, unbearable illness, and demands of ministry, this very special woman of God has stayed steady and unmovable in the face of adversity.

Marriage is a tapestry of varied roles, commitments, and responsibilities. I have observed Iris fulfill every challenging task with optimism and grace. I now observe how our daughters imitate her qualities and look to her for advice and counsel. Our grandchildren as well can't seem to get enough of their Nana.

This very special woman is my wife of forty-one years, and I love her and thank God for her life. I treat her like a queen, and she treats me like a king!

—JOHN DELGADO
HUSBAND AND FRIEND

Dr. John Delgado is the president of Vision International Leadership Network, a Christian educational ministry training leaders all around the world.

INTRODUCTION

TODAY WE ARE inundated with tons of counsel and advice for married couples. Much of it is inconsistent and unscriptural, but some of it is very helpful. As I thought and meditated about the counsel and advice I want to share with today's married and prospective couples, I kept coming back to my own experience and the confessions of many couples experiencing painful and difficult situations in their relationships. In our marriage seminars, my husband and I are witnessing an alarming increase of unhappy marriages and chaos in too many Christian homes.

Perhaps your marriage is wonderful, healthy, and stable.

Perhaps it's just so-so; one day it's up and one day it's down.

Perhaps it may be like so many today—hanging by a thin string, ready to dissolve any moment.

I have confidence that the counsel in this book will equip and guide you to find solutions that will empower you, with God's help, to enjoy a wonderful and healthy marriage. Some of you may need a total marriage makeover, and that too is possible.

Through these pages you will find my own candid advice about marriage and the real-to-life experiences of couples facing the onslaught of Satan's attacks. This advice is based on personal experiences throughout my forty-one years of marriage with the same complex and wonderful man. You will find out about my effective plan of action and my specific prayers and thoughtful on-purpose habits. My intention is not to tickle your ears or make you feel good, but to prepare you for the sudden tornadoes and devastating floods Satan is always looking to bring upon God's marriages. When you build your house upon a firm foundation, Satan can blow all he wants, but he won't be able to blow your house away.

You will be able to relate to many situations and, at the same time, learn about what makes a good till-death-do-us-part marriage and many of the things that can destroy it. I intentionally keep my writing style simple and to the point. It is my intention that no matter at what level, status, or profession you find yourself, you will be able to understand the practical, no-nonsense advice found among these pages.

I believe that you too can have a wonderful and fruitful marriage. I also realize that many couples are hurting because of different types of abuse, and healing is necessary before change can begin. I pray that you will be able to find healing through this counsel.

CHAPTER ONE

MARRIAGE TODAY

Is your marriage strong enough to withstand today's epidemic of divorce?

Let marriage be held in honor (esteemed worthy, precious, of great price, and especially dear) in all things. And thus let the marriage bed be undefiled (kept undishonored); for God will judge and punish the unchaste [all guilty of sexual vice] and adulterous.

—HEBREWS 13:4, AMP

As a BABY boomer, I remember hearing many of my friends complaining about the fights and abuse they were facing in their homes. My best friend confided that her parents were too busy to listen. Many of my junior high school friends expressed their fears of their parents divorcing. In my own home there was a constant uncanny fear and lack of freedom to express love and enjoy life. Instead of love and commitment, my father ruled the home with control and abuse, driving the siblings to develop hatred and contempt at an early age. I vowed at the age of eighteen that when I married, it was going to be different.

My own children, labeled *Generation X*, born in the 1970s could have been victims of my own upbringing. Instead I have chosen a different path, one that has led my family to wholeness. It is a known

1

fact that many of the Generation X parents defy their upbringing and pour everything they have into giving their children everything they didn't have, no matter how great the sacrifice, including divorce. To allow our own marriages to end up in a bitter divorce is allowing the curse of divorce to continue affecting each generation.

Members of today's generation believe they are on a different wave, a wave to save their children from experiencing the heartaches of their own parents. But it comes at a great cost—they are neglecting to protect and nourish their intimate relationship with their mate. Yes, children are better educated, fed, clothed, and pampered, but at a great price, one we will see manifested in our next generation. Many parents will look back and notice the pain their crumbling relationships inflicted on their children, pain they did everything to avoid.

Today's married couples are trying to avoid divorce for the sake of their children, but not for the sake of their mates. Sadly, when the nest is empty, there will be two strangers wondering what went wrong. Going on behind closed doors in too many homes today, yes, even Christian homes, is:

- Lack of commitment
- Crisis...fear...depression
- Lack of order...permissiveness
- Criticism...shame...condemnation
- Unsatisfied marriages...selfishness
- Infidelity...cheating...divorce
- Financial crisis
- A single-mom boom
- Pregnant teens

- An obsession with self and possessions
- Sensual dressing...body makeover craze
- Rebellious, unsupervised children
- Online porn and resultant sexual addictions
- Child abuse...molestation...incest
- Bisexual relationships
- Mental issues...insatiable desires
- Lack of communication and affection

Yes, all these different symptoms and tragedies are facing our society today. Marriage is under assault. Our children are at risk. The news media reports right in front of our eyes every day confirm the downhill slide of family values. No one is escaping the onslaught.

My intention in writing this book, especially for young couples, is threefold:

- Care and maintenance
- Prevention
- Rescue

If you will apply these principles and counsel *at whatever stage your marriage is in today*, I promise they will be effective and powerful to build up and to bring change.

LUKEWARM VALUES

A national poll conducted by Gallup shows that while Americans still hold on to some traditional moral values, they have validated immoral behaviors that are self-satisfying.[1]

The words *self-satisfying* got my attention. The need for

self-gratification can blind a person from noticing the needs of other people, especially those of loved ones. Many marriages are suffering because of lack of satisfaction and passionate love for each other. When a Christian becomes *lukewarm* in his walk with God, everything else turns tepid, and indifference begins to settle in (Rev. 3:16).

During our Christian conferences and marriage seminars, altars get filled to capacity with couples asking for divine intervention for their marriages. Hands go up everywhere when we offer prayer for children with problems. It's everywhere—crisis, chaos, brokenness, abuse, instability, prayerlessness, lack of respect, rebellion, dissatisfaction, unfaithfulness, frivolous divorces, and on and on. It is on your turf and on my turf.

The other day I was sitting at a food court in the Festival Flea Market in South Florida, the kind where everything is new and under air conditioning. As I looked around at all the people busy shopping and eating, I noticed many elderly couples, mostly Jewish, talking, laughing, and carrying on, and many enjoying their potato knishes and kosher hot dogs. As I thought about it, I asked myself: What makes these couples so different from so many other couples we know and meet every day?

As I pondered and savored my last bite of knish, I turned to my husband and said, "Honey, I guess what makes the difference in these couples from so many others we know whose marriages are in crisis is their value system."

He readily agreed and added, "Most of them have a healthy fear of the Lord. They were brought up memorizing scriptures, saying prayers, and following specific biblical traditions that have impacted their lives, as well as the lives of their children and grandchildren."

I believe our moral value system has deteriorated and continues doing so at an alarming rate. Our values will determine the destiny of our future, the strength of our marriages, and the values our children will respect and inherit.

Today's modern family defies everything the Bible teaches about love, honor, and respect for the marriage covenant.

> The traditional family was once regarded as two married parents, 2.5 kids, a dog and a white picket fence. However, the rise of the "modern family," made up of single parents, partners living together, or even older parents who have moved in with adult children shows that the definition of family is changing—and with it, how families spend their leisure time.[2]

SATAN'S PURSUIT OF YOUR VOWS

God's design and purpose for marriage was for a man and woman to have a lasting and satisfying union to nurture and rear healthy offspring. God established marriage as the only institution to nurture a family before sin came into existence. To take care of loneliness, God created woman to be a helper and companion to man (Gen. 2:18) as well as to procreate and prevent fornication (Gen. 1:28; 1 Cor. 7:1–2).

Marriage is the most sacred of all vows or oaths a man and woman will ever make. It is not like a promise that can be forgotten or broken. When a couple makes this vow before God and witnesses, they are making a sacred commitment and covenant "till death do us part," not "till divorce separates us." *Vows remain intact even if the marriage is full of problems*—and too many are experiencing warfare because of all the excess baggage they refuse to release to Jesus. Satan is in hot pursuit of your marital vows. He can't break the vows, so instead he diligently works at sowing dissension and strife until he succeeds in breaking up the marriage.

Too many couples just walk away from their vows. God's blessing is upon those who keep "an oath even when it hurts" (Ps. 15:4, NIV). Millions of people who divorce annually in our society are literally walking away from their commitment, but they will have to answer to God. Lacking wisdom, way too many couples have married foolishly, making promises they are unable to keep. God is in the business of healing and repairing the things that are broken and messed up. God's storehouse of provision and blessing is available to all those who dare seek healing and keep their vows.

Today's thinking is that maintaining a lifelong marriage is impossible. Self-fulfillment and gratification are exploiting the desires of so many of today's younger couples, and they refuse to endure a little pain in their relationships. The moment a difficult problem arises, they are out the door. Satan is extremely busy devising sinister schemes against the sacred bond of marriage.

Being raised in New York, I was very saddened, as I know millions of Christians were, when I read the following article, titled "Empire State Strikes Against Marriage."

> After a days-long deadlock, the New York Senate voted…to legalize same-sex "marriage" in the Empire State….But where same-sex "marriage" is recognized, the citizenry have been silenced. All seven jurisdictions that have same-sex "marriage" on the books share a common theme: Citizens have not been granted a say in the matter. Instead, courts and elected officials have effectively declared themselves first and final arbiters, imposing an expanded definition of marriage on millions of people and thereby hammering away at the very foundation of our society. Government, the people are told, knows best. The future of marriage should be the people's to decide. No one who values God's blueprint for sexuality as only between one man and one woman within the bonds of marriage should sit back as state legislators and federal courts try to co-opt and expand this sacred institution. Otherwise we could soon see the trademark homosexual rainbow stretch from coast to coast. And "Lesbian, Gay, Bisexual, and Transgender Pride Month" would take on a whole new meaning.[3]

EPIDEMIC OF UNHAPPY MARRIAGES

The decline in moral values in this nation has given rise to an epidemic of unhappy and unsatisfied marriages and unstable children. This nation has sanctioned and encouraged no-fault divorces and same-sex marriage. Christians just look the other way. We have allowed the ungodly to dictate what we can and cannot say. We have allowed sensual programming and entertainment to invade our homes. We have allowed our young girls to get abortions. We have allowed prayer to be taken out of our schools. We have allowed prayerlessness to sneak in on us—replaced by our social media enjoyment. This list could be a mile long.

You may say, "*We* haven't allowed this!" But *our passiveness* has allowed it! We all sit back and allow a small percentage of outspoken, demon-possessed advocates and activists to squelch our belief system and God's principles for a healthy, successful, and happy marriage. Again, all children are at risk, which means that our future generations of married couples are also at risk. I can almost feel God's tears rolling down my face.

To be honest with you, we need to pray for a spiritual overhaul in our personal lives. We need God's divine intervention, or we are going to be run over by our enemies. Only those standing firm on God's solid foundation will be able to overcome the onslaught of pervasiveness and outright sin that is invading every fiber of our society.

WATCH OUT FOR THE LITTLE FOXES

If you are married and happy, reinforce your personal life by paying attention to the little foxes that will come to steal your happiness. Stay anchored to Jesus Christ your Savior, and build yourself up in your faith. Pay specific attention to your spiritual life, and pray powerful warfare prayers. We are in a war. Our struggle is not with humans but with demonic entities that are constantly looking for an open door to sneak in and begin their work of destruction. If your marriage is healthy and solid, invest some time in another young couple and teach them what you practice and know.

Don't fall asleep. Declare boldly, "Satan, you can't have my marriage!" "Satan, you can't have my children!" "Satan, you can't have what belongs to me!" Don't just stroll through la-la-land. We must tread upon evil spirits that come to steal our substance and our faith. *To tread upon* is warfare action terminology. It means to trample, walk, crush, and march. To be effective, you have to put on your spiritual cleats!

You can't remain passive in your daily spiritual walk. To conquer something difficult, you must engage the enemy before he engages you. Trample and crush evil with the Word of God and with your prayers. God will do the rest. We must do what God expects from us to love, obey, and believe that He will fight our battles. Then He will enable us to do the impossible things. Only then can you have your cake and eat it too.

David couldn't kill Goliath with a small stone, but with God's help, he did! The disciples couldn't feed five thousand people with a child's lunch of fish and bread, but they did! By himself, Jonah couldn't escape from the belly of the fish, but after three days he did. Peter couldn't walk on water, but he did. Lazarus couldn't walk out of the tomb after being dead for four days, but he did. I couldn't be healed from the torment of child abuse, but with God's help, I was. My mother couldn't stop my father from carrying out his threat of massacring all the family, but her warfare prayers did. No situation is too tough or too far gone. God's satisfying blessings have conditions, and a holy God will not bend His rules for anyone. You can trust Him to turn the most difficult situation into a miraculous blessing.

GENUINE LOVE IS NEEDED

Without the genuine God kind of love, today's marriages are at extreme risk. Genuine love means an open, honest, sincere, unaffected, candid, pure, real, and unpretentious kind of love. Christ Jesus models this kind of love for us. The love of Jesus in us is the superglue that keeps a marriage together and satisfied.

Solomon expresses his enraptured feelings about the mystery of love in the Song of Solomon. We should read some of these passages slowly and think about the intentions of God when He created us with deep desires to love and be loved. Sometimes I think about this and realize how shallow our expressions of love are toward our mates. We think that by saying, "I love you, honey," we cover all the meaning of true love. Solomon uses romantic expressions that leave us lacking in expression.

> Ah, I hear my lover coming!
> > He is leaping over the mountains,
> > bounding over the hills.
> My lover is like a swift gazelle
> > or a young stag.
> Look, there he is behind the wall,
> > looking through the window,
> > peering into the room.
> My lover said to me,
> > "Rise up, my darling!
> > Come away with me, my fair one!"
> > > —SONG OF SOLOMON 2:8–10, NLT

You may say, "Oh, this is poetry at its best." I truly believe the language of love is poetic—we just don't take the time to practice and come up with some genuine, original phrases that will knock our socks off. As I write this, I just tried a different phrase on my husband: "I love you, my handsome lover; I'm going to take you for a spin."

His eyes got big as saucers, and he gave me a big old grin and said, "I'm ready! Where are we going?" This is one way of awakening a boring relationship.

Today's married couples, especially the younger ones, are so wrapped up in their jobs and the world of social networking and media entertainment that little time or patience is left to nurture the relationship, and even less to spend quality time with children.

I was immensely glad to see my daughter's post advising other couples on Facebook on her recent fourteenth wedding anniversary: "Today I celebrate a fourteen-year anniversary with my honey. Don't give up on your relationships. Remember the 'crazy in love' feelings you started out with, and do whatever it takes to keep them or ask God to help you get them back. God is our glue. It's all worth it!"

Now that's awesome advice for any couple at any stage of their marriage. Without demonstrative love in a marriage, life is like a cold overcast day. Love is affection, tenderness, desire, intimacy, kindness, enthusiasm, and so much more. Today's marriages are faced with tremendous opposition of evil forces. But always remember, that if you belong to God, you have a supernatural covering and awesome spiritual power at your disposal. If you're not there yet, keep reading, and make a decision to work at your marriage. Make it a safe haven for all your passions and marital needs. Put God first in your life, and all good things will be added unto you (Luke 12:31).

Today's Step-Home

Many couples go through a devastating divorce, and later they remarry. Some may have the added responsibility of stepchildren. Children of divorce or separation become the *victims*. The word *victim* means, "fatality, prey, loss, sufferer, wounded, harmed, help-less, somebody hurt and used for sacrifice." As you can see from all these sensitive meanings, a precious victim comes in with many defenses to overcome.

It is not uncommon in today's marriages to hear couples place the blame on stepchildren for disrupting their lives. The modern family is so busy and occupied that dealing with the emotional issues of a stepchild often seems like too much work. On the other hand, the new parent may have little or no experience or tolerance for dealing with all the new concerns that arise on a daily basis.

Heaps of books have been written about the uphill trauma of dealing with divorce and the unexpected trials of raising stepchildren. I've prayed for many couples who are trying to cope and, at the same time, keep their sanity. Rarely do I meet a person who is truly happy raising someone else's children. If you find yourself in such a situation, recognize that the fatherless and motherless have a special place in God's heart (Ps. 10:14, 18).

Recognize that stepchildren are the flesh and blood of and closely knitted to your spouse. Ask for God's help, and avoid becoming bitter or having a bitter stepchild. *Pour yourself into your family, and God will pour Himself into every aspect of your lives.* Marriage won't work when you draw separate lines.

I highly recommend my book *Satan, You Can't Have My Children* as a spiritual warfare guide that will help you train children effectively.[4]

C. M. Ward said, "It is not divorce that destroys families, but bad marriages."[5]

Chapter Two

INVESTMENTS FOR FAITHFULNESS

Invest before bankruptcy knocks on your door!

Know, recognize, and understand therefore that the Lord your God, He is God, the faithful God, Who keeps covenant and steadfast love and mercy with those who love Him and keep His commandments, to a thousand generations.

—Deuteronomy 7:9, AMP

And He said, I will hide My face from them, I will see what their end will be; for they are a perverse generation, children in whom is no faithfulness.

—Deuteronomy 32:20, AMP

Today's marriages will not survive spiritual bankruptcy unless a couple starts depositing quality investments into their relationship. To *invest* means, "to participate, devote, finance, capitalize, deposit money in a bank, contribute effort to something, and give something particular quality."

Don't wait until your health and youth start fading away. This book is intentionally about marriage and spiritual warfare. A Christian marriage without the practice of spiritual warfare is at great risk. Satan may not bother a non-Christian marriage because he knows that Jesus is not their Lord, but he delights in tormenting a Christian marriage, always attempting to steal their faith and joy.

INVESTMENTS TO SPARK A FIRE OF FAITHFULNESS

There are some very important investments that a couple can make in their marriage covenant that will spark the fire of faithfulness for a lifetime of happy marriage. Begin to make these investments in your own marriage!

Make an investment of always speaking truth and making right confessions.

Speak the truth in love to each other, and be transparent. Don't pretend. Be honest. The secret here is to do it in love. Even if your spouse gets angry, God will honor you. When you speak truth, you will have nothing to hide. God always honors and rewards truth.

> Rather, let our lives lovingly *express truth* [in all things, *speaking truly*, dealing truly, living truly]. Enfolded in love, let us grow up in every way and in all things into Him Who is the Head, [even] Christ (the Messiah, the Anointed One).
> —EPHESIANS 4:15, AMP, EMPHASIS ADDED

We make the choice of either speaking creatively or destructively, positively or negatively, in doubt or in faith. Our choice will determine the measure by which God will answer our prayers. A negative confession will hinder a person from receiving the blessing. But if we speak with faith and unwavering confidence in God's Word, then we open the channel of heaven's resources to meet our needs.

Making a right choice, holding on to it, and confessing your faith will cause "the power that works in us" to do tremendously and abundantly above anything we can ask or imagine (Eph. 3:20). The key here is the power that we have operating in us. You may be a novice, but when you speak truth and confess God's Word, the power of God in you will equip you as a roaring lion against the attacks of the enemy.

Many times our tongues will get us in trouble. There is a time to speak truth and a time to remain silent.

> There is a type of eagle in Turkey which preys upon the crane, a bird which is very prone to chatter and squawk as it flies along. The eagles will often mark the approach of a flock of cranes by the noise they are making, and will then swoop down and make the talkative birds pay dearly for their carelessness. The birds that survive these attacks apparently learn wisdom, for it is not uncommon to find the older cranes picking up a stone before they take to the air, and holding it in their beaks while they are in flight. With a stone in their mouths they have to fly silently, and therefore safely. There is a lesson there for us![1]

Make an investment of time.

Plan for times of refreshing and enjoyment. Making time for each other communicates love and desire. Too much work and no play will eventually cause friction and arguments. Don't allow busyness and boredom to settle in. The bustle of life will never disappear, but an unattended marriage could disappear.

Make an investment of listening.

Not listening is a major complaint among discouraged couples. Lack of attention belittles your partner. Really listen. Some couples stay busy watching TV or working on their computers while their spouses are speaking to them. Constant lack of focused listening will cause a spouse to opt not to communicate when important and necessary. The art of listening is learned. The person has to purposefully pause from his or her own activity and thoughts to intently listen to his or her spouse.

Good listening habits will create good understanding and atmosphere. Satisfying relationships are developed through good listening. I've heard many divorced people confess that the reason they fell into temptation was because someone else was willing to listen. You may also wonder why some children develop a hermit attitude. Often it is because no one is listening to them. As they get older they realize, "Mom and Dad didn't hear a thing I was saying. They were always too busy or were pretending to listen."

Many couples feel the same way—they have no one with whom to share intimate feelings. Not listening is positioning oneself into a danger zone. Conversation is considered one of the top needs of a woman. She may be waving the red flags furiously, but the other person is looking in the opposite direction. Eventually, love walks away.

What do women find inspiring? Words. Women are blessed with an auditory system that won't quit. That's why women are always saying, "He doesn't talk to me." Men, talk to her! Don't worry about what to say; just say something. She'll keep the conversation going for both of you. Discuss what's on your mind without sounding argumentative. Tell her you love her. She should never question whether or not you love her. I have never counseled a couple in which the man spoke lovingly, kindly, and graciously to his wife, only to have her abandon him.

Listening and good communication will set the pace for a good sexual relationship.

Make an investment of prayer.

Prayer will be your most fruitful investment. Prayerlessness will cause weakness and spiritual parasites to eat away at your relationship. Communicate in the spirit with your Abba Father. Allow the Holy Spirit to be your friend and your teacher. The practice of prayer must be a requirement for every Christian home. Without it, all the windows and doors are open for the thief to come in. "Watch and pray, lest you enter into temptation. The spirit indeed is willing, but the flesh is weak" (Matt. 26:41).

Your personal growth depends on prayer. A healthy body needs food, and a healthy spirit needs prayer. In God's presence the battles are won. Prayer creates in us a thankful spirit, and a thankful spirit brings joy into a marriage.

Make an investment of giving God the glory.

Learn to give God the glory (exaltation, credit) for all the big and little things in your life. Glorify Him because He is our Creator and Lord of all. When we give God glory, it brings Him pleasure. We are literally saying, "God, we give You all the honor and all the glory. We exalt Your magnificence and awesome splendor. Hallowed (sanctified, respected) be Your name." Go ahead and amaze yourself by glorifying God. He will be more than delighted to bless you and your home. Glorifying God also opens the door for appreciation and thanksgiving, whether our baskets are full or almost empty.

Kathryn Kuhlman said it this way: "Giving God the glory isn't something one learns from books. It has to be learned by walking with Him through the shadowed valley. If one lives on the mountaintops all the time, he gets hard and leathery, insensitive to the finer things of life. Only in the shadow of the valley do the tender crops grow."[2]

Don't fret about the shadowed valleys and the storms and trials that are sure to come. Learn to practice the habit of giving God glory, and soon you will be saying, "God is good, all the time."

Make an investment of healthy communication.

Lack of communication was the number one complaint in two surveys I did, one on Facebook and one during a marriage seminar. My question was: What is the biggest problem in your marital relationship? Out of seventy-eight answers, forty-nine said communication was the number one problem.

The ability to interact in conversation about any subject is the fundamental principle of marriage. Communication isn't always verbal. Attitudes are expressed by a frown, a shrug, a smile, and these can be powerful. We may sense annoyance even if the words are approving. Without communication, there can be no well-being in a marriage.

Communication means, "contact, exchange of information, message, access, and rapport." Many experts confirm that lack of communication and understanding will create a rift that will eventually affect every other aspect of a marital relationship. If making contact and exchanging information with your spouse doesn't happen consistently and with understanding, the marriage will eventually suffer, because communication is like prayer.

We communicate with God in the spirit and with our spouse in the natural physical realm—face-to-face. *Prayer unites us to Christ. Good communication unites us to our partner*, creates healthy growth, and stabilizes misunderstandings.

A colleague and Christian family counselor explains it this way: There are at least six versions of every spoken communication:

1. What the speaker intended to say

2. What the speaker actually said

3. What the speaker thought he said

4. What the listener wanted to hear

5. What the listener actually heard

6. What the listener thought he heard

In order to determine clarity, a person must ask for feedback. Feedback helps to ensure that the message sent is the message received. An example might help illustrate. I say to my friend, "Gee, that's an interesting shirt that you're wearing."

My friend responds, "Well, if you don't like it, stick it in your ear."

Apparently my friend has heard a message from me that says, "I don't like the shirt," when in reality I do. The way to deal with that is either defensively or, hopefully, if I'm a good communicator, asking for feedback. "Gee, what did you hear me say by my message?"

He might respond, "You don't like my shirt."

"Oh, no, that's not what I meant. I like your shirt; it's very nice."

At that point we are both clear about the meaning of my message. We have both interpreted it the same. Without feedback, we can have fights, distortions, or misinterpretations, which lead to conflict in relationships. The foundation of marriage is its communication system.[3]

Gut-level conversations are necessary between couples. They must be open and honest. Feelings and emotions must be integrated with the intellect and the will. In gut-level communication, emotions must be made known to the other person in such a way that they understand what you mean. Many times, keeping your feelings inward after a negative episode will result in animosity and bitterness.

Positive communication is possible and reachable, but like a beautiful garden, it must be cultivated and improved.

Make an investment of sustained interest.

Lift each other up by showing interest in the things you both enjoy. Whether it's dancing, playing golf, fishing, going to a concert, walking and shopping in the mall, watching sports, or cooking, do it together or allow each other to enjoy it. Husbands, enjoy her collections, her decorations, her outfits, her taste in art, and her body. The key here is to support each other and enjoy doing things together. If fishing is not your preference, don't complain if your spouse goes fishing. But the next time do something you both enjoy. The man who enjoys fishing and does it all the time, ignoring his wife, is acting selfishly and inconsiderately, especially if she has already voiced her displeasure.

Loving your spouse is all about pleasing each other continually without ceasing. Just as praying without ceasing is possible, loving your spouse without ceasing is also possible. It's an attitude, a lifestyle, and an awareness of atmosphere. Learn to discern when an evil spirit is causing strife or if it's your own selfish attitude.

You take a major step in personal growth when you love your spouse more than you love yourself.

Make an investment of changing a bad habit.

> As long as a person can tolerate being the way they are they are not likely to change. They may admit they need to change. They may even say they want to change…but *until the pain of remaining the same hurts more than the pain of changing, people prefer to remain the same.*[4]

Change means, "to break, exchange, alter, convert, transform, revolutionize, adjust, amend, substitute or replace, remove or to make different." All these meanings are action words. Action is necessary to break a bad habit. When we exchange a bad habit for a good habit, everyone will notice, not only your spouse.

You may be dealing with a bad habit of anger. Flying off the handle every time something goes contrary to the expectation is something that prevails among many Christian couples. A Christian may not indulge in alcohol or do drugs, but anger has always been a dominant hindrance to many. Not only does anger disrupt relationships and induce fear in children, but also many studies reveal that anger can affect a person's health.

Dr. Gary Smalley explains that anger eats away at a person's health. "Inside the brain, the decision you make to harbor negative feelings toward others can set off a series of physical events you would do well to avoid. When a person becomes angry, his body goes on 'full alert.' When the inner brain gets the message that there's a stressful situation out there, it doesn't ask questions—it reacts. Your body can easily release as many chemicals and disrupt as many bodily functions when you are angry with your spouse as if you're being attacked by a wild animal."[5] Dr. Smalley also describes the greatest problem of all. Using the scripture in 1 John 2:9-11, Smalley teaches that continual anger toward another results in losing the ability to live in God's light. He says: "Being angry with our brother pushes us into darkness—completely isolated from the light of His love."[6]

A *habit* is "an addiction, a pattern, and a practice." The more we practice something, the better we get at it and the more we do it. A bad habit becomes an instant reaction to negative situations. Instead of finding a solution, anger lashes out in defense—defenses that cannot be justified by God's Word.

Bad habits produce bad decisions. To break an addiction, it will be necessary to take action, get help, go after the root, yank it out, and make a decision to stop taking the drug of anger, lying, controlling, overspending, or whatever it is. Your marriage will grow stronger every time you defeat a bad habit and replace it with a good habit. This too is spiritual warfare.

Make an investment of forgiveness.

In his book *Discovering the Laws of Life*, John Marks Templeton says: "Some of us choose to hold on to old and painful thoughts as though they were treasures. We seem to cherish memories of imagined or real mistreatment, or slights, and to forget the good and helpful things people have done for us, the good health we have been blessed with and the many successes we've enjoyed.... Try to hold this simple truth in mind: yesterday is gone. No matter what happened then, it's over. We can't go back. Tomorrow may never come, so the present may be all we have.... A mind that is occupied by positive thoughts is a beautiful garden, free of the weeds of negativity."[7]

Taking control of your thought life, rather than seeing yourself as a victim, will heal you of unforgiveness. When we forgive, we release the person(s) who hurt us. Unforgiveness is like hate; it's an attitude that constantly invades a person's mind with thoughts such as: "Leave me alone." "Don't come near me." "I can't stand you." "You hurt me too much." "I would rather see you dead."

I've been there. I wanted to see my father dead many times because of the abuse I experienced as a young child. Healing came when I chose to release him by asking God to forgive him and heal my own heart. I chose to forgive my father when I understood the meaning of John 20:23: "[Now having received the Holy Spirit, and being led and directed by Him] if you forgive the sins of anyone, they are forgiven; *if you retain the sins of anyone, they are retained*" (AMP, emphasis added).

I realized that God knew what He was doing when He exhorted us to forgive others their trespasses. If I had decided not to forgive my father, I would have retained his sins in my own mind and body, haunting me on specific and unwelcome occasions. *Oh, no! I must be set free from this!* What a revelation that was for me. I looked up the word *retain* and found that it means, "to recall, keep something, recollect, remember things, hold something within." Walking around with the chains of shame, guilt, and condemnation is enough to sink anyone to the ground.

Once I made the decision to forgive, I was set free. It was that simple. The memories didn't disappear, but the sting and hatred dissipated with time. When the memory invades my privacy as a flying dart from Satan's hand, I send it right back to the enemy's turf, flying on this powerful scriptural truth: *I am free forever from condemnation* (Rom. 8:1).

Make a powerful investment in your personal life and for your marriage—forgive! Go to an altar and leave your baggage there. Have someone pray for you. Be set free. I was, and today I'm enjoying a wonderful harvest of peace and wholeness. We may not be able to change someone's behavior, but God can.

Booker T. Washington said, "I shall allow no man to belittle my soul by making me hate him."[8]

Erwin W. Lutzer said, "'Whatever you don't forgive, you pass on!'...Without forgiveness, there is no hope of peace and tranquility in our relationships."[9]

Make an investment of faith.

In the life of faith, many times you'll have to leap before you look! Faith is having confidence in God. He is a rewarder of all who seek Him with persistence. When you pray and believe God for something, such as healing, don't give up and start doubting just because you don't receive the healing right away. Keep thanking God until you see the healing manifested.

If you're praying for an unbelieving spouse, don't give up. Continue loving the person and hating the sin. Keep thanking God for his or her salvation. Spiritual warfare is tenacious. You should never give up. God has promised to perform His Word. In our walk with God, we cannot be afraid of the boisterous wind. Faith is always based on the promises of God, never on natural considerations. When we allow ourselves to be ruled by the natural conditions, we will never see a miracle.

Exercising our faith every day is like walking on water with Jesus. "He [Jesus] came to them, walking on the sea, and would have passed them by" (Mark 6:48). Look at this meaningful sight. The Master was walking upon the water in the midst of a raging storm, intentionally meaning to walk right past His almost drowning disciples. He had no intention of helping them until they pacified their fear and released their faith. Jesus is still waiting for a lot of us to release our faith and trust Him for the miracles.

Faith is your assurance that God cares for you and your situation, and He will do something about it. He needs your active faith and confidence as well as your obedience. Whether your unbelieving spouse decides to walk out or allows God to transform his or her life, God will sustain you as you continue standing with unwavering faith. Remember that God is your rewarder. In the midst of a hellhole you can make it!

My mother taught me tenacity. Her faith was unwavering in the midst of tribulation with an ungodly husband. She nurtured nine children and steadily and consistently took the rudder of her ship and steered it toward God. She didn't allow her husband's indifference and controlling menace to interfere with her convictions. For a long time after I was married, I wondered why Mom decided to stay in that situation until my father passed away. Looking back, I can understand that without my father's sole income she couldn't have made it on her own. Faith was the only positive assurance she could stand on—and she did.

I am amused and marveled when I see the final results of Mom's extraordinary faith. She reared a healthy bouquet of beautiful, gifted, intelligent, and God-fearing sons and daughters. *In the midst of a hellhole, your faith will steer your ship in the right direction.* Faith is your title deed of the things you hope for (Heb. 11:1). Faith is born in prayer and released by faith.

Have you ever wondered why Christ spent so much time in prayer? It was not that He lacked anything. But it was simply that through prayer, the faith that was in Him became activated, alive, and irresistible. And in this prayer-born faith, He went out to heal the sick, hush the storm, feed the multitude, and show Himself master of all that was in the world—showing that the greatest function of prayer is to create faith so that we may not be weak but strong, and may gloriously overcome the world (Luke 18:1, 8)![10]

Make an investment of examining yourself.

Erwin W. Lutzer says: "Here is a bit of wisdom that will help you through many difficulties: When something goes wrong in your marriage, rather than think that your spouse is at fault, try taking responsibility yourself. Your first thought should be, 'I am at fault!' One partner usually bears greater responsibility for the failure of the marriage, but seldom is one partner wholly responsible. A root cause in marital strife is that we seldom want to 'own our own stuff,' as the saying goes....Search your own soul to grasp your part in the conflict."[11]

To *examine* is to, "inspect, test, investigate, and study something." We have a hard time examining our own motives and actions. The blame game comes first. I find that humility is one of the greatest attributes that we can possess. A prideful spirit will not allow people to truly examine themselves. When strife enters your marriage, ask the Holy Spirit to put His flashlight into your heart to test if there is anything you need to own up to.

> Examine me, O Lord, and try me;
> Test my mind and my heart.
>
> —Psalm 26:2, nas

Chapter Three

DIGGING OUT DESTRUCTIVE, HARMFUL ROOTS

*Learn to recognize the invading parasites that
will choke the life out of a marriage.*

Beware lest there should be among you a man or woman, or
family or tribe, whose [mind and] heart turns away this day
from the Lord our God to go and serve the gods of these
nations; lest there should be among you a [poisonous] root
that bears gall and wormwood.

—Deuteronomy 29:18, amp

Just the other day, my husband and I sat with a dynamic
couple and listened to the reasons why they were on the verge of
a breakup. The husband, a minister with a thriving congregation,
anxiously described the discontentment in his heart. He claimed
he had become coldhearted and was no longer interested in pur-
suing or fighting for his marriage. Twenty-five years of marriage had
produced three lovely daughters, now adults. This union had also
produced many good relationships, helped many other couples with
marital problems, and enabled many young people to feel loved and
useful. Many good things were an extension of this vibrant and well-
rounded couple.

ied and took mental notes, I inwardly asked the Holy
scernment and wisdom to give sound advice. My hus-
l intently as he searched his heart for answers. We asked
ourselves what the real root of this disintegration and sudden desire
to end it all was on the part of this man.

UNCOVERING THE HIDDEN ROOTS

Roots are always hidden. But knowing the root of a problem is necessary to help a broken marriage. Some of the more prominent issues
that came out during our discussion with this couple were:

- Lack of trust and confidence

- Mishandling of finances

- Dishonesty and covering up evidence

- Repetition of the same offense

- Jealousy of coworkers

- Suspicion

- Harshness

- Discontentment

On the outside everything seemed good and normal. People
were getting saved in the church. Growth was steady. The wom-
en's group kept growing and thriving. Leadership was being developed. Everything was gearing up for a phenomenal breakthrough
and expansion of the ministry.

> Sir, did you not sow good seed in your field? How then does
> it have *tares*?
>
> —MATTHEW 13:27, EMPHASIS ADDED

Let's get back to the roots. When lack of trust and discontentment invade a relationship, immediate intervention is necessary to identify the root causes of the problems, or an invasion of demonic parasites will take over. In this situation, the wife had been warned many times by her spouse: "Don't keep using your credit card to make purchases you can't pay for at the end of the month. Consult with me when you really need something that your monthly allowance doesn't cover. If you need extra money for food purchases, let me know. Don't borrow money from your friends or relatives. Be honest with me, but don't allow your credit card to max out and then hide it from me."

And he added, "She goes through frequent spells of jealousy of my office or volunteer female workers."

This entire episode had been repeated several times. Frustration was mounting like a ferocious wildfire that couldn't be contained.

The first lady had other explanations as to why her husband was unhappy. Her face withdrawn and her eyes averting contact with my eyes, she proceeded to agonizingly paint a picture of discontent and unbelief about why her husband wanted out of their marriage.

Some of her defensive reasons were: "I have to keep using my card because I run out of money to buy groceries. He doesn't realize that everything has gone up in price. I barely have enough money to take care of my hair appointments and personal things. I hate to beg him for money because he just doesn't understand. And...he seems to be paying more attention to the attractive divorcee who works in the office than to me. I have confronted him with this situation, but he tells me that I'm imagining things and that their relationship is strictly normal and befitting a minister. He claims that the habitual hug and peck on the cheek is customary with all the other women in the group. I just feel there's something different about this one. He seems to come alive around her, and he even sends her e-mails keeping in touch and giving her encouragement—something he normally doesn't do with anyone else of the opposite sex.

"When it comes to our children, he wants to have the last word about everything that concerns them. He corrects me instead of correcting them. I am really confused about what he expects of me. One day he's happy, and the next day he's moody and unreasonable. The more I try to please him, the more he demands of me. So now I stick to my ministry with the women, and I don't bother with anything else. I don't know what else to do."

Now can you see some of the root causes of discontentment starting to burst out from the bottom of this situation?

The following is some of the counsel we gave this couple, beginning with advice for the wife:

1. *Admit the fault.* She had to admit that this was not the first or second time that the same situation and argument had evolved in their relationship. She also admitted that each time the same vicious cycle was repeated, it strained their relationship even deeper.

2. *Admit the problem with overspending.* She needed to admit that she had a problem with overspending, hiding the evidence, and then lying about it. The remedy we suggested was that she be willing to agree that her husband take her credit card, pay it off, and that she do without it until she was ready to make a real commitment.

3. *Admit the problem with jealousy.* She also needed to admit that she had a problem with jealousy. The spirit of jealousy can destroy a relationship and quench the fire of love and joy. This spirit stems from lack of confidence and trust. These two things had been lacking in this marriage for a very long time,

and they are extremely necessary for the success and well-being of any relationship. We recommended that they pray together and cast out the tormenting spirit of jealousy, followed by positive confessions and a determination to make drastic changes wherever necessary.

Then we gave some advice to the husband:

1. *Don't neglect the sensitive areas.* We recommended to the husband that he keep in mind the sensitivity of his wife in the area of jealousy and that he do everything in his power to avoid the appearance of over-exuberance whenever young women were in his presence. We counseled about the danger of communicating with this particular divorcee via e-mail or otherwise and his need to use proper protocol.

2. *Learn what things actually cost.* Another recommendation was that he pay more attention to the expenditures such as groceries and toiletries. Everything has gone up in price; what cost ten dollars a few months or weeks ago may now cost fifteen dollars.

We recommended many other things, but only time will tell if this marriage, like so many others today, will overcome the chaos and turmoil that have been covertly eating away at the roots for so many years. Repentance, forgiveness, accountability, and specific change would be necessary to save this marriage.

After a while we received an e-mail from the husband saying that things are more peaceful among them, but that there's *a hole in his heart*. He also said that if the same situation is repeated again, he's walking out of his marriage. For this couple in active ministry, there is a lot at stake. Not only is the inheritance of their children on the line, but also so is the stability of many other couples who look up to them.

A few more months went by, and then I received another e-mail from the wife saying that the relationship between them is much better. They were able to have a powerful discussion, listen to each other, argue some points, come to an agreement, and apologize to God and to each other. Of course, the ball is in each other's court. Both have a responsibility to keep their part of their spoken agreement. They will experience a battle of their wills and, sometimes, feelings of contempt, but the price to pay is great. As leaders, they must establish their boundaries and be accountable to someone mature and stable in their walk with God, someone with a track record they can look up to.

I believe women in general have a lot of intuition, and the jealousy part could have been caused by something that was truly brewing in the husband's heart even though nothing had happened. In this case, the husband taunted the wife with the idea that the woman his wife was jealous of was attractive and very fit and that the e-mails and phone contacts he had with her were for counseling. The problem with this situation is that if their marital problems continue, the man could easily find himself attracted to the forbidden fruit, and if he doesn't fall with this one, he could fall with another. The heart-problem has to be confronted and dealt with through counseling and confession.

Will this marriage survive? Only if they both choose to continue making the necessary changes and adjustments, become intimate and completely accountable to each other, and allow God to continue healing them before the hole in the heart becomes inoperable. Is it possible? Of course it is!

Too often we see the red flags waving all over the place and refuse to make changes. The end result is always a breakdown of communication and lack of intimacy, which leads to a hole in the heart.

There are many reasons why a woman could have a problem

keeping within the limitations of an allowance of money and then lying about the overspending. In this case she was brought up in an affluent home where she didn't have to work and had everything her heart desired. Now she found herself unable to buy whatever at any time. Even when there is enough food, clothing, vacations, and beauty salon visits, when a person gets into the habit of shopping all the time and desiring what someone else has, it can end up becoming an addiction. When an addict becomes desperate, he or she will lie, connive, borrow, and hide the evidence.

Things like impulsive shopping, watching television all day, getting carried away with collectibles, an insatiable desire to read romance novels or eat impulsively, an infatuation with pornography, an addiction to antidepressant medications, or anything that can become addictive can drive a person to do many dishonorable things.

In some cases where the woman is the dominant and controlling figure in the marriage, the husband is reduced to a puppet who brings in the money, and the wife supervises every penny, most of it going to addictions after bills get paid.

Making a decision to divorce may seem appealing and tempting, but it will not be the awesome liberation many people expect it to be, especially when children are exposed and traumatized by it. Divorce is a ripping apart of two people who had become one flesh. The results are always devastating.

Lou Priolo, a divorce counselor, writes: "Most [who divorce] have come back in one way or another and acknowledged that the suffering they experienced was much greater than they initially thought it would be.... They invariably told me that if they had it to do over again, they wouldn't."[1]

Harmful roots of criticism and ridicule

Criticism is rated as one of the most pernicious spirits to invade the sanctity of marriage. To *criticize* means, "to express disapproval, disparage, assess, censure, pass judgment, complain, condemn, blast, lash out, nitpick, and pick holes." To criticize your spouse or children is to condemn and belittle them. Millions of people walk around ashamed and feeling unworthy because of someone who has criticized and humiliated them, never looking back to say, "I'm sorry; please forgive me."

To *ridicule* is to mock or make fun of a person. You will find people in all walks of life wandering around with a broken spirit. These are evil roots that, if allowed to remain in a relationship, will bring discontentment and eventually separation.

I like what Kay Arthur says about a broken spirit: "Never, never break another person's spirit. You will lose him! You will lose her! Don't ever make your mate—or anyone else—the brunt of your jokes. Never ridicule. Never mock. Be very, very careful with barbed humor. Your words, so lightly spoken, may remain in an individual's soul until his or her dying day. Ridicule and mockery is cruel and kills communication. As Solomon wrote, 'A brother offended is harder to be won than a strong city' (Prov. 18:19 [NAS]). If you have offended your mate or another in this way, go and ask forgiveness."[2]

In Numbers 12, we find that God inflicted the prophetess Miriam with leprosy for criticizing Moses. Criticism and murmuring go hand in hand—they both cut down and accuse a person. Many relationships, especially in marriage, suffer in agony and silence because of a critical spirit. When criticism is allowed to persist and the offended person is never redeemed or restored, it can cause a spirit of bitterness and low self-esteem to take root. I've seen many young women devastated and affected by this form of mental abuse.

The person who constantly nitpicks, murmurs, and criticizes his or her spouse is leaving an open door for demonic attacks to inflict the entire family. God looks at a critical murmuring person just as He looked at Miriam. One of the reasons why we encounter so many defeated and anemic Christians is because they are suffering with the curse of leprosy. Leprosy is a skin-and-nerve disease. Spiritual leprosy may not physically kill you today, but it will make a person spiritually dead. Repentance and forgiveness will be the only way out of this one. "Wow," you may say, "I never saw it like this!" Millions of people walk around hurt and deprived of joy because of these offenses.

In a marital relationship, some of the most common criticisms are these:

- "You're too fat now. Why don't you lose weight? You look awful."

- "Your breasts are too small; why don't you get a boob job?"

- "Your nose is too big."

- "You're a bad cook."

- "Can't you do anything right?"

- "Your legs look like drumsticks."

- "I can't believe you're so stupid!"

- "You're dumb."

- "You're ignorant."

- "I can't believe I married you."

- "When are you going to learn to do things right?"

- "Stay home; I don't want to be seen with you in public."

- "You can't even get it up. You're like a lump in bed."

- "Sex is no fun with you."

You may think of many more. This kind of personal criticism attacks the core of a person, and that person may never rise above or recover unless divine and professional intervention is applied. Only forgiveness and reconciliation will initiate the process of healing in a relationship that has been assaulted by this kind of behavior.

Harmful roots of unresolved guilt, shame, and condemnation

This sounds like Satan's trio of affliction. What is guilt? It can be described as a worried conscience or an awareness of wrongdoing and a feeling of remorse. We feel guilty for actions we regret and feel responsible for. Many victims of sexual abuse, whether an incestuous relationship or perpetrated by a pedophile, feel guilty and dirty for involvement in situations for which they were not responsible.

Sexual abuse can take many forms and can be defined as any sexual activity—physical, verbal, or visual—engaged in without the consent of the victim. It can be physically or emotionally damaging. Sexual abuse seeks to exploit a person in order to meet another person's sexual or emotional needs. Guilt caused by abuse will cause confusion in the person's belief system.

Shame can be described as a feeling of unworthiness or a painful emotion caused by embarrassment or an offense. We feel guilty for wrong things we do, and we feel shame when we realize who we have become. Shame is an inner force that debilitates your understanding of God's love for you.

Condemnation is disapproval and blame. It tends to put a legal sentence on the person, making him or her feel condemned for doing something bad.

> Therefore, [there is] now no condemnation (no adjudging guilty of wrong) for those who are in Christ Jesus, who live [and] walk not after the dictates of the flesh, but after the dictates of the Spirit.
>
> —ROMANS 8:1, AMP

Guilt, shame, and condemnation are closely related to each other. It is Satan's intention to keep people bound by these emotions, which cause agitation and disturb the well-being of relationships.

Why do I think these emotions are so important to overcome? There was a time when I personally had to deal with all three harmful emotions. I was told in counseling that I had to cope with the emotions of child abuse. But I learned through the years that coping was not good enough. *Coping is managing and surviving. My desire was to be set free.* I discovered that my freedom came by allowing the Word of God to wash me clean as I applied it to my life consistently. You must make a radical decision to be set free of these three emotions. Today I testify that I am completely free, and coping is out of the question.

> My son, attend to my words; consent and submit to my sayings. Let them not depart from your sight; keep them in the center of your heart. For they are life to those who find them, healing and health to all their flesh.
> —PROVERBS 4:20–22, AMP

The Word of God is like a river of living water that brings cleansing and forgiveness. When you apply it to every aspect of your life and remain consistently connected to the Holy Spirit for wisdom and understanding, you will mature and understand the spiritual warfare we are involved in. Make a list of powerful scriptures and pray them aloud every opportunity you have. The Word of God is alive and active. Don't remain passive in your passion for the things of God. Allow the Spirit of God to have preeminence in your heart.

Your self-worth is connected to your freedom. There is lots of information written by professionals that will give you a deeper insight into the mechanisms of these evil spirits, but my intention is to open your understanding to the fact that you can be set free. Your freedom will also set others free.

Harmful root of nagging—a testimony

The following is a real testimony of a young wife, crying out for help. I begin with my letter to her after her confession to me of a problem with nagging.

"Hello, Marcia: It was good hearing from you although this was such a difficult confession for you to make. These are critical times, and so many young couples are ending up in divorce. I thank God that you chose to confide in me. This means that you're willing to work this out and consider making changes. You will need to make some quick positive decisions if you want this relationship to be restored. For the time being, let's forget about Fred, and let's concentrate on you. I will not defend him; I only want to concentrate on you right now.

"First of all, the devil is beating you up with condemnation. The enemy's condemnation will take your eyes off of the answer and the solutions. You're not a hypocrite; you just haven't had enough teaching or a good example of how a marriage functions and the things we do in ignorance that can kill a relationship. From reading your e-mail, I notice several things that YOU have been doing that have not helped your marriage and situation. You write:

1. "'I constantly nag him because he tends to be very irresponsible when it comes to his finances.'

2. "'For the past few weeks I have been nagging him about that and also coming home late.'

3. "'During the last few months I have been telling him that he is not the same—always in a bad mood and easily upset.'

4. "'But I don't know what I've done wrong because to me, all was going well.'

5. "'We have also drifted away from God, and I know
that plays a big factor in this. I feel like a hypocrite.'

"Marcia, I see a pattern and a very big problem here that affects many marriages—constant nagging! The Bible says in Proverbs that constant nagging and complaining of a woman is like a constant drip of water on a tin roof or a leaky faucet. It drives a man away. 'A nagging spouse is a leaky faucet' (Prov. 19:13, THE MESSAGE).

"Attacking a man's self-esteem is instant warfare. It will definitely have a bad effect on the relationship. Telling a man that he's not the same anymore and that he's changing will only reinforce the behavior. It will cause him to come home later and later so that he doesn't have to face the nagging.

"Drifting away from God is a major cause of personal and spiritual problems. The woman is the one who sets the spiritual thermostat in the home. She is also the motivator. When a man has no impulse or is passive, the woman should take over with a positive take-charge attitude and make decisions that will honor God and bring stability to the family. One example is getting everybody and everything ready for church on Sunday morning.

"I am speaking to you from my heart, my own marital relationship, and from many years of counseling young couples. Having a relationship with the Lord is a must! Tendencies such as nagging will dissipate with time as you apply God's principles. It is the plan of the enemy to destroy you, your marriage, and your children. You will never notice the enemy's tactics when you're away from God. *You will only notice the enemy's plans and tactics when the Holy Spirit is involved in your life.* When you're disconnected from God and finally notice all the bad stuff happening, then you realize, 'Hey, but I don't know what I've done wrong because to me, all was going well.'

"OK, Marcia, I don't want to hammer your head. I just want to put some positive counsel into your mind to help you make some quality changes that will positively affect your marital relationship.

1. "Go before God and repent for neglecting your relationship with Him. Ask Him to forgive you and to help you in this situation. Ask Him to cover you and your family with His love and favor. Be specific and ask the Holy Spirit to guide your steps and to help you practice the language of love with your husband. Declare that you want to be a peacemaker. Please use these prayers I have enclosed as a guide and believe in your heart that there is still hope and your marriage can be restored. [Please refer to my website www.crownedwithpurpose.com and click "Powerful Prayers" for more information.]

2. "Call Fred and ask him to forgive you for all the nagging you have done. Confide that you have thought the situation over and realize you acted in anger and ignorance. Tell him you love and need him and desire to restore the relationship. A man must feel needed in a relationship. Tell him you want to start fresh. Don't preach to him or talk about God or church. That will come later when things are better between the two of you. God has to be a part of your lives if the marriage is going to grow stronger and healthier.

3. "Find a good Bible-based church where both of you feel free to worship—not a dead, boring church. Be patient; give him some space and time to think. But please don't wait too long to take my counsel and put it to work. I know this works. This move should be a priority. My husband and I will counsel with Fred.

In the meantime, trust God and cast fear out of your heart."

Ending of this story: We spoke with Fred. *His biggest beef was that he was finding less and less to admire in his wife.* As time went by, she was getting careless, had gained a bunch of weight, was always too tired for intimacy, and griped and nagged about everything. He said that unless she made a complete turnaround and became as sweet, nice, considerate, fit, and intimate as she was when they first started off, he was out of the marriage.

Less than two years into their marriage, Marcia kept complaining and nagging, even though she followed some of my counsel and they became involved in a good church. Nagging was the harmful root that triggered the lack of admiration and intimacy in this relationship. Sadly, this marriage became another casualty of the divorce epidemic.

Harmful root of jealousy

Jealousy means, "envy, suspicion, watchfulness, distrust, and possessiveness." There will come a time in almost every woman's life when she will feel jealous of another woman. It may be because she feels her husband is paying too much flattery to another woman, or because of competition, or because Satan introduces a spirit of jealousy. Men as well are not exempt from this spirit of jealousy. A spirit is a supernatural entity. There are good spirits, such as the Holy Spirit, and there are demonic spirits such as the spirits of jealousy, suspicion, fear, torment, infirmity, lying, and many more. They all have one thing in common: disruption. If a person allows them entry, they will cause havoc and disappointment.

> …the *spirit of jealousy and suspicion* comes upon a man and he is jealous and suspicious of his wife…
> —NUMBERS 5:30, AMP, EMPHASIS ADDED

How you deal with jealousy will determine if you regain your peace or become obsessed with the situation.

I remember that not too long ago my husband was paying compliments to another woman about my age. Although it was harmless, my mind interpreted the compliments in a different way. Every time they met, my husband would repeat the compliments with a big grin or a slow whistle and say, "You look great!" I would go home and stew. Sometimes I got into a bad mood. Mind you, she was an older attractive minister who divorced when she was younger. After the third time this happened, I decided to face my husband with the issue. I thought about it first, telling myself I could either confront him or spill it out, matter-of-factly, without showing my true emotions. I decided to stay calm.

I confessed to my husband, "Honey, I'm jealous of this woman. Every time you see her, you pay her compliments that seem overly enthused. I don't know what to think." The moment I got the last word out, my husband jumped out of his chair and took me into his arms, gently hugging me and telling me how much he loved me and was sorry that he had caused me to become jealous. From that point on we both learned a valuable lesson. It never happened again.

What if I had reacted differently and confronted and accused him? My story would be different today.

Jealousy is a foul, unclean spirit whose sole purpose is to cause havoc, torment, and destruction. The spirit of jealousy can also drive a person to commit murder because jealousy has torment.

My counsel is that the moment you feel yourself getting jealous of your spouse, immediately talk about it in a calm, nonconfrontational but serious way. Both husband and wife need to take quick action to stop the behavior causing the jealousy. If action is not taken, the tormenting spirits will pile one on top of the other, and you will deal with not just one spirit but many.

Harmful root of unhealthy mother/daughter relationships

Some of us have a good relationship with our mother, and some don't. One of the reasons why many grown-up men and women continue to have a bad relationship with their parents is because of spoken words that created resentment, fear, rejection, or a negative memory that still lingers in the heart. In the case of a young woman, she marries and moves away, but every time something adverse happens, there is Mom again, with her nasty comments and wise remarks. The pain never goes away, and healing doesn't seem like an option. Many problems in marriage are the result of a woman's low self-esteem, which was caused by an insensitive parent. Though I'm dealing here with mother/daughter relationships, this is also true of mother/son and father/son/daughter relationships.

Following are some of the negative comments some mothers make that I've heard in counseling sessions:

- "You were a mistake from the beginning. I didn't want to get pregnant, and I was mad and angry when I did. You were a pain from day one!" (These words cut to the gut, especially when they are brought up when an unfavorable situation develops. The victim feels like a failure all his or her life.)

- "Oh, I can't believe you had a miscarriage. You're just a little too old to have children; you disappointed all of us!" (The victim is thinking, "Hey, how about me...hello! Does anybody care about me? I am devastated!")

- "Why did you marry that man? Don't you see that he's never going to amount to much?" (That constant criticizing and nitpicking from a mother can drive a good marriage apart.)

- "You should go on a diet; you're getting fat. How do you expect to find a good man?" (Wow! This one is really prevalent in many relationships, and it causes daughters to build up resentment and long-lasting bad eating habits. Instead of losing, they gain.)

- "Oh well, you never finish what you start! You're so undependable and unstable!" (This is a big put-down. It causes the victim to become an excuser—if mom believes it, it must be true.)

- "You should be like your sister; she does things right the first time." (Having a favorite son or daughter always causes the "not so favorite" to become resentful and to develop a low self-esteem.)

- "You're not a good mother. You need to put your foot down...etc., etc." (Meddling in a couple's child-rearing decisions always causes friction, contention, arguments, and frustration in the entire family.)

I know you can think of something negative your mom or dad said that has stayed with you through life and still has an adverse effect on you, especially when it's time to get together for a family reunion. It makes you feel like you are never good enough to please your mom or dad. In fact, you dread the family reunions and special events, and many times you get too sick to go.

MY COUNSEL

Love your spouse and children no matter what.

It doesn't matter if they are beautiful, ugly, skinny, fat, sanguine, melancholic, choleric, or phlegmatic. It doesn't matter if they are quiet and a little slow or rambunctious and hyper. As a mom or a single daughter who hopes to marry some day, it is our responsibility to gain knowledge about child-rearing. Read all the good books by well-known authors and those with PhDs in the field. Read, read, and read.

Stay positive.

Be positive. Speak positively. Think positively. Pray positive prayers. Go against the grain of your upbringing and break those habits of speaking and thinking negatively. Practice saying something positive to your spouse every day. You may not be used to it, but practice saying something confidently different that is not part of your nature or personality.

Speak words of affirmation.

Speak words such as:

- "I love you very much."

- "You're very special to me and to God."

- "You're gifted, and I have great confidence in you."

- "God will always help you."

- "Trust God and serve Him."

- "You can do it! Try again. Don't be afraid to fail."

- "You can count on me."

- "Your heart is in my heart."

- "I love you more than all the leaves on the trees and all the flowers in the field."

Wow, that sounds good, doesn't it! We all enjoy hearing these wonderful words of affirmation and praise. It makes us want to stick our chests out and put our heads up and straighten our shoulders. *Positive affirmations create the way for positive, creative, and well-adjusted men and women.* These are the kinds of words that great moms and dads instill in great children who accomplish great things in life. You too can be one of them!

Receive training.

Many of our moms had no previous training. All they had was the training they received at home from their own parents, and most of the time it was very inconsistent and cultlike. Some of our moms never received loving affirmations, kind words, good solid advice, rewards, or healthy hugs and kisses from their parents. Many of them may have been abused by their fathers, just as some of you may have been abused by your dad, a brother, a family member, or a stranger. Hey, I was there too! I know what I'm talking about. Abuse is not just sexual. It could be mental abuse introduced through hateful words or pornographic material and videos. It's like a vicious and repetitious cycle of curses and learned bad habits that keep haunting each generation. It is time for you to make a difference and break those awful and life-defeating habits and personality traits.

We reap what we sow. If you give love, you will receive love. If you hear kind words, you will learn to speak kindly to others.

START MAKING ONE CHANGE AT A TIME

If you're hurting and you have a lousy relationship with your mom or some of your family members, consider making some of the following changes:

- Ask God to help you forgive them.

- Forgive yourself.

- Put your head up and declare that you are the righteousness of God in Christ Jesus.

- Declare that you are chosen, beautiful, and equipped for every good work.

- Go to the next family reunion feeling wonderful, unafraid, fearless, and loving.

- Speak blessings into your life to break curses.

- Stop complaining.

- Read one scripture every day. Repeat it several times during the day (while you're driving, eating lunch, bathing, etc.).

- Make a list of the characteristics of your position in Christ. Memorize it and declare every day that you're the righteousness of God in Christ Jesus, an overcomer who is forgiven, chosen, justified, redeemed, and free from all condemnation.

CHAPTER FOUR

AFFAIR AND DIVORCE PREVENTION

Prevention starts with knowledge and action.

For the Lord, the God of Israel, says: I hate divorce and marital separation and him who covers his garment [his wife] with violence. Therefore keep a watch upon your spirit [that it may be controlled by My Spirit], that you deal not treacherously and faithlessly [with your marriage mate].

—MALACHI 2:16, AMP

D IVORCE IS NOW common, accepted, widespread, and happening in unprecedented numbers, affecting beautiful and not-so-beautiful men and women of all faiths and cultures.

What are some of the strongest reasons that drive a married man or woman to have an affair? This is truly a complex question, for there could be a myriad of answers. But I will share with you what I consider some of the top reasons that trigger affairs and eventually a divorce. All of my observations are based on literal cases of couples I personally know through counseling and others I know as acquaintances.

Lack of transparency. Accuracy, clearness, self-expression, lucidity, simplicity, clarity, exactness, and truth—all these words imply not telling the whole truth.

Transparency needs to begin during courting. If significant things are hidden, they will eventually come to the light and may disrupt a marriage relationship. Things such as addictions, abuse, prostitution, an abortion, a child out of wedlock, a felony, a divorce, a common-law marriage, existing debt, or lawsuits are important issues that need to be exposed before a couple enters into the sacred covenant of marriage.

Lack of transparency leads to lack of good communication. The offender only settles for bad communication such as backbiting, nagging, and arguments.

Carelessness. This includes lack of care, negligence, neglect, lack of attention, sloppiness, imprudence, lack of judgment, and lack of caution and wisdom. Many of these issues can become the beginning of the end of a marriage. And all of these issues can be corrected. A person who is careless and sloppy can learn to undo these character traits by incorporating changes and new habits.

Disrespect. This encompasses feelings of disregard, contempt, insolence, and impertinence (impoliteness, brazenness, and lip-service). The Bible is very clear about the need for honor and respect between married couples. Disrespect cuts to the core of a person. It causes brokenness of spirit. A mate will tolerate so much, and then one day he or she can explode.

Familiarity, which is awareness, ease, experience, informality, relaxedness, and casualness. Familiarity can lead to taking a person for granted, such as allowing our mind to think, "Oh, it's just my husband; I don't have to get fixed up. If he wants coffee, he can get it himself." The more we disassociate ourselves from our partner and become informal and too relaxed, the more distanced from each other we become. I find it is very important to be vigilant and aware of each other's needs. Dropping the ball can lead to losing the game. Familiarity can lead to neglect.

Control and manipulation, which means to maneuver, have power over, be in command of, rule, dominate, oppress, have a hold over, dictate, restrain, keep under control, keep in check, hold back, contain, monitor, check, regulate, inspect, limit, and restrict.

These irreverent spirits are rude and demanding. Any mate who has to deal with a controlling and manipulative spouse is a very unhappy and bitter one. Many remain in the marriage for a long time, but eventually they call it quits. A controlling woman can also be very sweet and accommodating when she notices there is trouble.

Loss of first love. Loss of any of these vital attributes—feelings of affection, devotion, attraction, passion, tenderness, keenness, dedication, zeal, enthusiasm, eagerness, wholeheartedness—will cause a fading away of affection. Without passion and love, there can be no tenderness or enthusiasm. Love between married couples has to be nurtured and pampered. We must feed it lots of good words, hugs, kisses, and intimacy. We must pronounce blessings and keep the relationship covered in prayer.

Unfaithfulness. This includes infidelity, disloyalty, betrayal, falseness, adultery, and deceitfulness. The Bible says, "…that a man should be found faithful [proving himself worthy of trust]" (1 Cor. 4:2, AMP). Infidelity is one of the main causes of divorce. Today, just as many women as men are being unfaithful to their mate. This trend is out of control, and children are the greatest casualties. My advice is that you do everything in your power to prevent an affair and divorce. Keep a watch over your spirit that it may be controlled by the Spirit of God. Carefully study every section of this book, and determine in your heart that you will have a powerful, blessed, and happy marriage.

Recently I did a study of ten women married twenty to forty years.

I was amazed at how *intimacy* and a *personal relationship with God* were the ingredients of the glue that kept their marriages together.

I addressed the following questions and have added my personal answers. I would like to challenge you to write down your personal answers and make a determination to reinforce your weak areas.

1. *What things do you enjoy doing together?* We take walks in the mall, go shopping, eat together, find time for intimacy.

2. *What makes you happy?* Peace, paid bills, grandchildren, saying, "I love you," worship music, basking in God's presence.

3. *What do you do in your private time?* I read, write, journal, pray, organize things, soak in the tub with special aromatic oils.

4. *How do you handle a stressful situation?* I keep my mouth shut, pray fervently, and later talk about it.

5. *How do you handle anger?* I look for the root, say I'm sorry, pray, and remember not to trigger it again.

6. *How do you handle sickness and disease?* I confess God's Word, talk positively, and take medicine.

7. *Do you like to read and study?* Yes, it is my hobby. I read inspirational books as well as biographies of great people and books dealing with health and nutrition.

8. *Do you set goals and see them through?* Yes, most of them. I set goals such as losing five or ten pounds. I prepare a weekly menu and stick to it. It really works.

9. *Do you like to cook and keep the house clean?* Yes, I love to do both.

10. *Do you go to church regularly?* Yes, every Sunday and for special meetings.

11. *Do you enjoy sex?* Yes, and I never say no, even when I don't feel like it.

Marriage is a partnership with many diversified responsibilities. We must choose to learn and put into practice everything that will make both partners fulfilled.

YOUR BODY IMAGE

It is important for you to feel good about your body, even when you don't like everything about it! Feeling good about yourself is something you won't be able to do if you don't love yourself first. *Too many of us have an inferiority complex.* We worry about our breasts being too small or too large, our legs being too fat or too skinny, our nose too big or too long, our butt too big or too flat, our teeth too crooked or too stained, or we criticize our body as being the wrong shape or the wrong height or weight. Our mate probably does not notice our imperfections until we keep pointing them out.

We are bombarded every day with the unrealistic need for body perfection. The latest surveys show record numbers of eating disorders, cosmetic surgeries, and total makeovers. The pressure is on not only to look good but also to look almost perfect. Study after study in this nation is warning us that obesity and eating disorders have become an epidemic. Young girls under ten years old are talking about diets, and young men and women are developing eating disorders such as bulimia and anorexia. We must take a critical look at ourselves and see if we fit into one of these categories of dissatisfaction.

There are so many physical things we worry about. But we must choose to examine our thoughts and emotions. We must learn what true beauty means according to our Creator. True beauty begins on the inside of the person.

If you're not content with some part of your body or have something you wish you could change, seriously take some time to think why you feel the way you do.

Let's take the breasts as an example—are they really small, or are you comparing yourself with other women with larger breasts, many with enhanced breast augmentations? If you're married, is your husband satisfied with your breasts as they are, or is it you who has developed an inferiority complex?

We can all find so many things to be unsatisfied about, but we must seriously think: "Will this make me happier than I am right now? What will be the next thing I'll want to improve?"

Everything is changing faster than we can keep up with it. Cosmetic surgeries are abounding, and so are the malpractice lawsuits. Everywhere we look we see and hear of something new to make you look fuller, younger, slimmer, and more beautiful. I am not against some of these new advances and techniques. What I see as a problem is the reason behind why we desire to do some of these radical changes to our body. Will you allow it to become an obsession? Will one procedure lead to the next, and the next, and the next?

God created you wonderfully made, whether you think so or not (Ps. 139:14, NAS).

MY COUNSEL TO YOU

I would be the first one to counsel you to get your teeth straightened and fixed if you need to. Your mouth is the one of the most important parts of your body. Skin problems of all kinds such as boils, acne, rosacea, blisters, or other things should be taken care of by a specialist. Other imperfections or annoying things about your body, such as weight, please do something about it.

If a breast augmentation is going to improve your appearance and the desires of your husband, then go for it. But if you're a normal size with lovely breasts, and having larger breasts has become an obsession, even for your husband, then you have a spiritual problem. I dare call it a problem of lust.

Feeling good and looking good is a choice, a choice that only you can make. No one is going to improve you. You must make the decision to plan some things, put them on your calendar, and follow through. These are things that are not obsessions but that tremendously improve your well-being, such as:

- A good healthy diet that includes necessary vitamins and supplements

- Time to rest

- A weekly beauty routine: exfoliation, ointments, healthy lotions, manicures, and pedicures

- A good haircut, scalp treatments, and hair color

- Exercise and hydration

- Good music, scented candles you both like

Some family members and even friends may criticize you or make embarrassing comments. But keep this in mind: you are the most important person to make a decision to plan for improvement in all of your weak areas and to follow it through.

Going back to the subject of breasts, every case is different. I've counseled with two young women about this. One said that her husband was insisting on her having breast augmentation. He wanted larger, voluptuous breasts. She had a beautiful B-cup when we had the conversation.

Another woman was a mom whose teenage daughter kept nagging her to please allow her to have larger breasts like her friends were doing. This surgery begins at approximately five thousand dollars and goes up from there. Nowadays many women sacrifice greatly to have this procedure done and often get into debt doing so.

The woman whose husband wanted her to increase her size to a D-cup went ahead and had the augmentation procedure. Is she happier? Not yet. Did it satisfy her husband? I'm sure it did. But let me tell you at what cost. This woman is not satisfied. Now she wants a larger butt, a totally flat belly, and a nose job. For many women it becomes a never-ending obsession, and it is never enough. How about the husband? Will he remain faithful and satisfied? Only time will tell.

The law of gravity tells me that as time goes on, our bodies start succumbing to the aging process. A race begins to see which breast gets to the waist first. There is no stopping it. We might as well learn to age graciously.

What happened to the mom with the insistent teenage daughter wanting larger breasts? Mom went ahead, put the cost of surgery on her credit card, and the young lady was happy. Not long afterward, the same young lady got married and divorced, all in the same year. What happened? What this young lady needed was some sound counsel on how to become a well-rounded, comfortable, self-assured young woman ready to face life, a home, children, and the unexpected storms of life. None of these very important principles were in place. Only: "Do I look good and sexy?" Looks are not everything; looks are only a part of the whole person.

As I write this counsel for you, I'm thinking of the many times I thought about how good it would be to have larger boobs. My husband would say, "If you want them, I'll pay the price. But if it doesn't bother you, it doesn't bother me. Don't do it for me! I love you just the way you are!" I finally decided that I would not take the risk.

Since then, a padded bra has worked wonders, and life has gone on as wonderfully as before. I am fulfilled, happy, and content, and my marriage gets better every day.

Honest! This spiritual mother writing to you is being very candid and straightforward. Learn to pay attention to the things that are important before an affair or divorce comes knocking on your door. Life is way too short!

There are some major things you must pay attention to such as:

- Your spiritual life

- Your thinking patterns

- Educating yourself about marriage

- The care and development of children

- Your mate and his needs

- Your nutritional and personal needs

- Finances and investments

- Care and upkeep of your home

There are so many things that are truly so much more important than your body looking sexy to you, your man, or other men. Whether you think so or not, a sexy body will draw the attention of other men and open the door to lust and lasciviousness.

Now what does *lasciviousness* mean? Here it is: "lewd, erotic, indecent, vulgar, coarse, arousing sexual feelings, marked by sexual desire, great eagerness or enthusiasm for something, the strong physical desire to have sex with somebody, usually without associated feelings of love or affection."[1]

ACCEPT YOUR BEAUTY

This subject is extremely important for you to comprehend. Please learn to accept yourself and your body the way God created you. If there are things you can do without surgeries to look and feel better, do them! If you have overweight issues, do something about it. Take this advice from this mom—the better you look, the better you will feel about yourself and everything else, the better your clothes will fit, and the more your honey will also enjoy you. Set a goal and keep it. You will be amazed at how easy it really is and how good it really feels.

Truly beautiful, natural-looking women are the exception. Most of us are average, ordinary-looking women who need to wear makeup, tuck it all in, and doll ourselves up to look good. Truly beautiful, peaceful, self-assured, confident, poised, and radiant women are also the exception. These are women who know their position in Christ and have a spiritual relationship that nurtures all their other relationships. Wow! This is the place to be and the woman you can become! The decisions you make every day will determine the outcome of the values and the inheritance you will leave your children for generations to come. Prevent an affair; learn to love your body by keeping it healthy and changing the things you can.

My daughter Kathy, who is married and has two boys, my grandsons, ages fourteen and seven, gave me the substance for this section. She's a great mom and wife. Her children are obedient, and her husband honors and respects her very much. I asked her, "What would you tell young married women that you consider is very important and has worked for you and will help them prevent an affair?" The following was her relevant response.

Fix Your Face

One thing that I make a constant effort to be aware of in my marriage is the way I greet my husband and children. If the first thing your spouse wakes up to is a grumpy complainer, it can make for an unhappy morning. Before you know it, you are arguing over nothing and just snapping at each other until one of you storms off to work waiting for the next victim to cross your path! That bad attitude just multiplies through the day. If you have children who get caught in the irritated cross fire on the way to school, that attitude just keeps on going. What a way to start the day! Been there, done that, and it really just makes you feel bad inside. When you finally calm down and think about it, honestly, you can probably trace right back to the moment that you let that mean, little, totally unnecessary huff and puff or comment slip out. We're all guilty of it.

And what about the expectations at the end of a long day? Do you or your spouse have to wonder what you will be walking into when you open the front door? We need to be sure that home is a safe place from the rest of the world. It's so important that we don't make our spouse feel like he or she is walking into a land mine when coming home, or that spouse won't want to be there. Those first few moments at home can set the tone for your whole evening. Do your best to make your family feel welcome and wanted. When your spouse or children walk in the room, do you want to be sure they know how busy or tired you are or how long your day has been? I want to make sure that each of them knows that I'm glad he or she finally made it home. I never want them to question if I'm happy to see them.

Fix your face, literally! I have found that making a real effort to be aware of my facial expressions when my family walks in a room can make all the difference. It's amazing how a big smile and a "Hey, baby" can defuse a flared-up husband who is walking in the door after having a horrible day at work. That little bit of effort can melt away frustrations that may have otherwise been thrown at me. Will it fix his problems? No. But now I'm not the enemy. I'm on his side, and he can breathe because he's home now. In turn, an irritated greeting will just add fuel to his fire, and in many cases, as I've seen, open the door for the word *divorce*.

It's definitely not easy at first, but we have to be conscious of our attitude and think about how we would feel if our spouse behaved the exact same way with us. Eventually our good attitude becomes effortless, and our family will respond positively. The same way we allow the snippy, grumpy attitudes to gradually become a bad habit is the same way we must allow the peaceful, happy greetings to become our new expected lifestyle. The change is amazing.

Another great reason to make peaceful greetings a habit is so that you can have better arguments. Yes, you read that right. When peace is the norm in your home, fighting and nagging don't fit in. That doesn't mean you'll never disagree with your spouse or be upset with him. It does mean that when there is a problem, you will be able to conduct yourselves like grown-ups and disagree, debate, and come to a solution.

I've seen people talk to their spouses in ways that they would never dare speak to a friend or stranger. Routine nagging and griping are a bad recipe for routine fighting and unhappiness. If you are fighting about anything and everything, then you're not being honest about what truly is bothering you. No one can hear you when you're yelling. A constant complainer gets tuned out. Bad attitudes suffocate the atmosphere. This way of life can't survive in a relationship where each person is truly making an effort to be kind to each other. I believe arguments and disagreements should be specific. When you deliberately show care and respect to your spouse on a regular basis, it is easy to voice complaints when they arise and to actually be heard. When peace and joy are your norm, your spouse will be ready and willing to help fix or change anything that would compromise that.

Kathy ended her comments by saying: "It really can start with a deliberate smile. I believe the face muscles just may be attached to the heart muscles."

This is what married life is all about—work, cooking, eating, cleaning, running errands, keeping appointments, and more work. It never ends. We must learn to do what we can do in the time we have by handling one situation at a time, staying composed, and creating some time for prayer and fun things. As you weave prayer throughout your day, you will find that God gives you wisdom and discernment to accomplish much more than you could without prayer. I have tested this over and over. It really works!

It doesn't mean you have to stop what you're doing and kneel to pray. No, it means that in the middle of cooking or cleaning, you hum a song, quote a scripture, make a confession, or thank God for strength. Prayer is talking to Abba Father. It could be anywhere, anytime, and about anything. It could be silent meditation. The key is to concentrate and not allow yourself to become negative or angry.

Too many of us frown too much. We create furrows on our foreheads from so much frowning. We start looking older than we are because we don't know how to relax or be at peace. The sad part is that the whole family learns to imitate each other. Before you know it, the husband has a long face, and when the children come along, they too learn to have a long face.

Like my daughter says, "Fix your face," and allow the joy of the Lord to radiate and invade your soul and your atmosphere.

Affair and divorce prevention should be something you consistently work on by improving your spiritual and physical lives on a daily basis. It must be a lifestyle of awareness and on-purpose, focused loving. Pride and selfishness cannot be part of the equation. The joy of the Lord must become your strength.

Chapter Five

KEEPING A FINANCIALLY STABLE HOME

Money matters

The Lord will open the heavens, the storehouse of his bounty, to send rain on your land in season and to bless all the work of your hands. You will lend to many nations but will borrow from none.

—Deuteronomy 28:12, niv

MONEY IS THE medium of exchange for everything. It is also indispensable. Becoming good stewards of our money demands that we acquire knowledge and understanding of money matters. Most young couples today don't have a clue about handling money. Problems in money matters are on the top of the list for reasons to divorce.

In my home we manage our finances properly by budgeting, and we also:

- Put God first (tithes and offerings)

- Budget for savings and investments

- Address *needs* first, not *wants*

These three priorities are just a suggestion; every situation is different. But my experience has proven that this combination works very well. Perhaps you need to clean up your slate first then follow a specific plan.

PAYING BILLS AND FILING

I give focused attention to finances and spending habits. My husband opens all the bills and is aware of all expenditures and bills due. We pay the bills on time by listing them on Excel and paying half at the end of the month and half in the middle of the month. I make sure that all bills are paid before the due date, eliminating late fees.

When both partners are abreast of all the expenditures and bills due, it is easier to live on a budget and be responsible to each other. When things are tight, we stretch the dollars by buying less, improvising, and eating on a budget.

I keep my files in such a way that when tax time comes around, everything is already in the correct files.

Unless the husband enjoys filing and keeping up with the bills and correspondence, I believe the wife should learn how to handle this task with excellence and without griping. It makes life easier to navigate. I've seen many couples in counseling complain about the mess in their billing and the fights over misplaced unpaid bills, bounced checks, and exorbitant late fees. There should be a designated place for billing, not in a corner of the bedroom or shoved into different drawers. Good and consistent habits are important when it comes to money.

Failure to develop a financial system that runs smoothly in the home has gotten too many marriages in trouble, causing many to end up in divorce. Lack of communication may be the number one complaint among married couples, but lack of financial prudence and meticulous attention to money matters is right behind it.

No matter who earns more, whether the husband or the wife,

both partners should have an awareness of all financial matters concerning the home. The Bible says that the man is the head of the home as Christ is the head of the man (1 Cor. 11:3).

WHO HANDLES THE MONEY?

In my home, my husband handles all the money, and I pay the bills. It works wonderfully for both of us. I have a credit card and a debit card. Since I keep the books, I am aware of how much money is available all the time. We consult each other about any expenditure over one hundred dollars other than groceries. We do not have separate accounts. My husband is aware of my hair and nail appointments, and I never have to ask permission for that. Like I said, when things get tight, we do without. Being accountable to each other on all money matters has created trust and confidence in our relationship. Problems in this area arise when a man is stingy, harsh, and irresponsible.

You may have another arrangement that works wonderfully and has instilled trust and confidence in your relationship. As long as both are in agreement and content when things are good and not so good, there will always be peace in the area of finances.

> For wisdom is a defense even as money is a defense, but the excellency of knowledge is that wisdom shields and preserves the life of him who has it.
>
> —ECCLESIASTES 7:12, AMP

GIVING

This subject may be the most important one you study about finances. Personally, when we neglect to make deposits into our storehouse (the ministry that feeds us the Word of God) and to the poor, we start noticing a decline in our finances. This lesson is so real in my own family that now two unconditional habits we follow are giving at least 10 percent of all our increase to the Lord and giving to the poor. God has never failed us. Our bills get paid in the good times and in the bad times.

> *Give, give, give*—many of us have heard the expression, "Giving is its own reward." While this is certainly true and more than reason enough to give, there's another aspect of giving that many fail to recognize. Giving is an energy that not only helps others, but creates even more for the person who is doing the giving. This is a natural law that is true regardless of whether the person who is giving wants or even realizes what is occurring.[1]

The Bible has a lot to say about finances. I would like to inspire you to become knowledgeable about what the Word teaches on this subject and to try putting it into practice, trusting God to perform His Word and bless you by supplying all your needs, above your expectations.

CREDIT CARD HABITS

I would like to recommend to young couples in debt that you do everything possible to *kick the credit card habit*.

> Credit cards are like consumer cocaine, and you can't kick the habit if you carry them with you. I concede that cutting up the cards can be emotionally challenging, but it's doable. Remind yourself that you can still buy things at your favorite stores with cash and enjoy the experience of shopping without the cards.[2]

Avoid covetousness, which leads to dissatisfaction and unreasonable demands. A covetous person also depends on borrowing to feed a certain lifestyle and is known for murmuring and causing strife.

Avoid comparison with other friends or family members. It can lead your household into poverty by trying to acquire what others have even when you can't afford it.

Avoid being broke all the time. Make investments and give to God and the poor, and you will never lack. Don't get used to living from hand to mouth with nothing left over. God intended for His children to prosper, not only in their souls but also in their pockets.

Start declaring, "Satan, you can't have my finances," while taking some positive action at the same time. Don't allow carelessness and the enemy to steal your substance and frustrate your marriage. Eventually carelessness, lack of budgeting, and debt will cause stress and depression. Most marriages under such strenuous pressures are unable to resolve conflict. The entire family suffers.

CHAPTER SIX

LOVE AND BLESS *OUT LOUD*!

*Mine your words as if digging
for diamonds and gold.*

Praise the Lord! (Hallelujah!) Blessed (happy, fortunate, to
be envied) is the man who fears (reveres and worships) the
Lord, who delights greatly in His commandments.

—PSALM 112:1, AMP

W E FUSS, ARGUE, nag, and express anger out loud—in front of
our children! Many couples I've counseled admit that after an
argument, many days and even weeks can go by in silence, remorse,
and outright anger. Intimacy during times of bickering and disagree-
ment is totally out of the question. One sleeps in bed and the other
on the couch or in the spare bedroom. This demonic atmosphere,
when it becomes a habit, is usually followed by the word *divorce*. We
are told that one out of every two marriages ends up in divorce.[1]
That is your neighbor and my neighbor.

Is this a common situation among many Christian couples? The
answer is yes, and too often. We *curse out loud* instead of *loving out
loud*! Our words and thoughts produce *life* or *death*. We choose! God
gave us the freedom to choose good or evil, peace or worry, contentment or depression, healing or sickness, order or disorder, wealth or
poverty, knowledge or illiteracy, and life or death. It is up to us.

Death and life are in the power of the tongue, and they who
indulge in it shall eat the fruit of it [for death or life].
—PROVERBS 18:21, AMP

The church I attend, Calvary Church in Irving, Texas, recently had
a "Love Loud" event where the people donated twenty-five cars and
over $35,000 worth of groceries as well as loads of children's clothing
and other stuff. The word got *out loud* that the church was *loving
loud*, and everyone was invited. The result was spectacular and over-
whelming. People came from all over the community, and the church
and grounds were packed out for multiple services. Many radio and TV
media outlets came to report the unusual contagious news, and multiple thousands came to witness and enjoy the *loving loud* experience.

My grandchildren love to come and visit our home. If my husband and I would allow them, they would spend every weekend with
us. They bounce in with big smiles and hugs, kicking off their shoes
and skipping to the refrigerator and pantry for snacks and drinks.
You can hear the house filled with their loud chatter and contagious
laughs. I keep a large corner behind my family room couch full of all
sorts of toys and games. I'm not bothered if my family room gets lit-
tered with toys, tents, books, and throw blankets. It is a joy for them
and for us. This is a pure example of loving and blessing *out loud*!

Our homes should be the place where we learn and practice to
sincerely *love* and *bless out loud*.

HOW DO WE LOVE LOUD?

- We smile and laugh and have good sex.

- We kiss and hug and embrace tenderly.

- We show kindness and serve each other.

- We go to church and pray together.

- We play and surprise each other.

- We listen to good music and shows together.
- We say "I love you" often and sneak up on each other.
- We don't criticize or shame each other.
- We listen to each other and communicate.
- We accept and please each other.
- We always say "I'm sorry" and forgive each other.
- We love each other silently and *out loud*!
- We never go to bed mad.
- We don't take arguments personally.
- We never accuse each other.
- We don't hide anything from each other.
- We never lie to each other.
- We always find something to admire.
- We love out loud and bless out loud!
- We shop, eat, and clean house together.
- We plan a vacation together.
- We pray for our children together.
- We go walking and driving together.
- We treat each other to our favorite little things.
- We sometimes bathe and massage each other.
- We speak blessings to break curses.
- We love *out loud*!

DO YOU FIND *OUT LOUD LOVING* HARD?

You may be one of the couples that find it hard to love and bless out loud. Let's consider some of the reasons why some couples find this hard.

New baby takes up all the time

Some young moms forget about intimacy and sex and complain all the time. They won't have dinner ready, and the house is always a mess. I see this happen all the time. In reality, many young mothers need help from their husband, especially if she works all day, picks up the baby and perhaps other children from day care, runs home to cook and clean, tends to everybody's needs, and gets up the next day and does it again. This routine can be very demanding and stressful. And to top it off, if a child is constantly sick or has special needs, the task becomes even tougher. Husbands need to pitch in and do their part, or this marriage will suffer the consequences of neglect and lack of wisdom. This too is spiritual warfare—carrying your part of the load. Before you know it, the children will be grown, and either you have nurtured a good strong relationship, or the entire family is falling apart. Young couples need to discuss these issues and implement a plan that works.

Husband won't pick up his mess or help with the kids

Nothing is worse than having to pick up a grown man's dirty clothes and shoes. As adults, this should not be an issue. A well-organized and smoothly running home takes much work. All family members must be involved in the process. Where there is chaos, there are always demons stirring up contention. Beware of the lack of commitment. It takes two to make it work.

Fights over checking accounts or a bad financial decision

Instead of one checking account, some couples have two and fuss all the time about who is paying what. A bad financial decision where things don't work out as expected is also a cause for arguments in a marriage. Read the section on finances in chapter 5, and don't allow this subject to be an open door for the enemy to bring destruction to your marriage.

Ethnicity problems

When a wife doesn't know or won't learn how to cook her spouse's favorite foods or enjoy their ethnic differences, trouble arises. Every effort needs to be made to please each other. If the decision to get married has already been taken, go ahead and learn to enjoy the challenges. Be committed to your vows. The same thing goes for the husband. Becoming one flesh means you enjoy everything about each other.

Hidden abuse issues in childhood that surface after many years

Sometimes the abuse may have been perpetrated by a close family member. This problem is so common that I believe every church should have a recovery class for abused people. Almost every family is affected by this topic. Just today a young married woman came to see me, tormented about the news from her teenage daughter who was raped by her uncle when she was much younger. Two months have passed since this information came to light, and she confessed that her relationship with her husband is now strained, there is no intimacy, and all they do is argue. During desperate situations like these, it is important that a husband be tender and understanding toward his wife. The feelings this mom has are feelings of guilt and condemnation, blaming herself for the abuse her daughter experienced. Healing and much prayer will be necessary for this mother and daughter to begin the process of restoration in this home.

An unsaved husband or wife

One spouse becomes a believer after the marriage and now has a hard time following along as usual. Or both married as believers and now one spouse has left the faith and is doing ungodly things that were not allowed when they first married. In either case, this situation can become a reason for disruption in this marriage. The believing spouse will have to be patient, follow the advice in the Word of God, and pray that the unbelieving spouse will come back to God. The Word says that the unbelieving spouse should not leave or divorce (1 Cor. 7:13). Verse 14 (AMP) says:

> For the unbelieving husband is set apart (separated, withdrawn from heathen contamination, and affiliated with the Christian people) by union with his consecrated (set-apart) wife, and the unbelieving wife is set apart and separated through union with her consecrated husband. Otherwise your children would be unclean (unblessed heathen, outside the Christian covenant), but as it is they are prepared for God [pure and clean].

These scriptures are pretty specific and straightforward instructions from the Word of God and should be heeded. Keep a good disposition and learn to love unconditionally. God always rewards the obedience of a faithful man or woman. God has you covered.

Death of a child

The death of a child can be very traumatic and trying for the entire family. Counseling and compassion are necessary to overcome. Instead of growing apart, a couple should draw closer to each other in such circumstances.

Adultery

The sin of adultery is a serious act of violation of trust, and it deeply affects the intimacy of the marriage relationship. This kind of betrayal causes mental and physical anguish. This sin is committed not only against the person involved but also against the spouse whose trust has been defiled. Many marriages never survive adultery. Forgiveness and reconciliation will be necessary to restore a damaged relationship. The perpetrator must take full responsibility for his or her actions, confess, and become accountable to a counselor or spiritual mentor.

My recommendation to couples who have not experienced this heart-wrenching experience is that you do all in your power to keep your love alive and follow some of the advice for the things to do to grow a powerful marriage, found in chapter 7. Don't slack off and think it will never happen to you. Stay vigilant and always alert to each other's needs. Love is action, not a feeling.

Barrenness

Almost every woman desires to someday have a child of her own. Surveys indicate that more and more women are unable to conceive. Though the problem is a little greater in women than men, 40 to 50 percent of couples are not able to conceive due to sterility in the male partner.[2] In men, smoking could be one of the most prominent reasons for sterility because it could lead to vasoconstriction. Frequent alcohol consumption, high blood pressure, cholesterol, diabetes, thyroid, rheumatoid arthritis, and other conditions can also be causes for sterility. Medicines used to treat these symptoms can affect sperm production.[3] Some women become barren after a miscarriage or difficult labor. There could be an obstruction caused by fear, grief, unrestrained passions, self-indulgence, lack of cleanliness, ovulation disorders, or blocked fallopian tubes problem. Treatment can be complex.

My counsel: You can find contentment by concentrating and getting involved in specific service areas that will bring joy and edify your marital relationship. In today's society many childless couples are pressured to adopt. It may be God's will for some couples to adopt, but it's not necessarily God's will for every childless couple to adopt. God will give you the strength and peace to remain totally happy serving God and others. If the Lord is not leading you to adopt, don't do it. When you adopt a child, you also receive the trauma and transferred spirits of the child's original parents. You must be ready and knowledgeable to understand the issues that will arise, and then be willing to get spiritual help. I've seen many couples go through extreme emotional duress trying to figure out what *they are doing wrong* when in fact it's what came wrapped with their beautiful bundle of joy.

Gay son or daughter

Today it is not uncommon for most families to be affected by a sibling or relative who decides to turn to a same-sex relationship. There are many things I can say against this subject, including what the Bible has to say about it. But instead I will limit my thoughts to married couples who are battling with this issue in their own household. When I was a teenager, I realized that one of my brothers had gay tendencies. We couldn't figure out why and how it happened. As I got older, I realized that something happened to him as a young boy that opened the door for an unclean spirit to influence his thinking and his emotions for the rest of his life. I've done some investigation on this subject, and I'm aware of medical studies that claim homosexuality is a mental disorder, an unhealthy disease-ridden lifestyle and others that say it is an inborn genetic predisposition.

My counsel: My mother loved my brother unconditionally. She was merciful, kind, understanding, and prayerful. We all learned to love our brother no matter what. Even though he never told us what happened, we know he attended a Catholic prep school, and from conversations he had with another brother, we were able to put two and two together about abuse that may have transpired by an overseer. If you have a child displaying these tendencies, please delve deep and get help. God is able to deliver and set a person free from all bondage, no matter how deeply rooted it may be. This is not a genetic issue or disease; this is a demonic spirit that invades a person through an abuse or the perverted sins of a parent or ancestors. Today my brother is able to enjoy family reunions and keep his family bonds because God's love rules in our lives and we did not allow this issue to separate us.

Other issues

There are many other conditions we can list that are reasons why couples find it difficult to display their love for each other, such as:

- Inherited curses

- A rebellious child

- Wife has intimacy issues because of past abuse

- Frigidity and fear of intimacy

- Erectile dysfunction due to illness

- Ignorance due to legalism and strict religious upbringing

- Overweight issues

- Perfection freak

- Workaholic

Loving out loud and loving unconditionally takes sacrifice and a want-to attitude and disposition. We all can do it if we try. If any of these or other conditions are affecting your ability to demonstrate active and powerful love, please get help from a Christian counselor before it's too late.

CHAPTER SEVEN

HOW TO GROW A POWERFUL MARRIAGE

*Things we do all the time to protect
and enjoy our marriage*

Love never gives up. Love cares more for others than for self.
Love doesn't want what it doesn't have. Love doesn't strut,
doesn't have a swelled head, doesn't force itself on others,
isn't always "me first," doesn't fly off the handle, doesn't
keep score of the sins of others, doesn't revel when others
grovel, takes pleasure in the flowering of truth, puts up with
anything, trusts God always, always looks for the best, never
looks back, but keeps going to the end. Love never dies.

—1 CORINTHIANS 13:4–8, THE MESSAGE

THE COUNSEL IN this chapter contains some of the things my husband and I do personally in our home and with our children and grandchildren to protect and enjoy our marriage. Use this as a checklist and see how many things you can check off as things you also practice. On those things you are unable to check off, consider trying one of them each week, and then observe the results.

I learned some of these principles from my dear mother, who experienced living with an ungodly, abusive husband. Some things

I learned from attending church, Bible studies, and women's conferences. Many other things I learned from reading good books written by professional counselors and men and women of God. And many other things I observed from watching mature happy couples.

I had to put everything good I learned into practice. Action was necessary for victory. I was naïve and unschooled in the business and practice of marriage and child rearing, just as most of our young couples are today. My first year of marriage was turbulent. I was doing so many things wrong and causing dissension and strife in our home. My husband was also impatient, disorderly, and abrasive with his dislikes. We were so opposite in our personality traits that a true miracle was needed to overcome.

Courtship and dating are usually a time of bliss and noncommittal. During this phase of friendship you can only see superficially. You never see the inner workings of the person. It reminds me of our relationship with God; we don't *know* Him until we get deep into the practice of His presence.

Allow this counsel to disciple and instruct you. My objective in listing the personal things that have immensely helped to form and edify my own marriage is to teach you how you too can learn to have a powerful marriage. You won't be able to say, "Satan, you can't have my marriage," unless you are doing everything possible to please God first and allow the Holy Spirit to teach you understanding.

I want you to look at these examples with an open-minded approach to learn and apply this counsel. Please don't think for a moment that I am boasting or showing off, because I consider myself blessed to have a satisfying and healthy marriage. This journey has cost me many sacrifices and self-discipline. When my husband and I started out forty-one years ago, we were green, inexperienced, and as opposite as day and night. My husband is very energetic and friendly. He has an I-can-do-it type of personality. I tend to be more reserved, with an I-don't-know-if-I-want-to-do-that personality. I am also a peacemaker. Being opposites has tremendous benefits. It doesn't matter what type of personality God gifted you with, you are able to perform with excellence when knowledge, wisdom, and understanding take priority over natural senses.

I am conveying this message with the heart of a loving and tender spiritual mother who desires that you too may have a fulfilling and strong happy home, abounding with God's blessings. I have learned to be content in all situations, to never hold a grudge, and to discern evil spirits when they interfere in our relationship. I have taken time to study, learn, and accept who I am in Christ Jesus. Having confidence gives you a better foothold on Satan's devices against marriage. For this advice to work for you, your spiritual position must take priority over your physical position. *This is a lifestyle of commitment!*

Practicing this valuable counsel has freed me from self-pity and regrets. My aim every day is to nourish my spirit before I nourish my body. I do this by reading a portion of Scripture and praying for direction, protection, and wisdom. I consider myself blessed and totally free of all condemnation. I want you to experience the same. These are the things my husband and I do in a consistent and focused manner.

BEING THE BEST YOU CAN BE

I keep an eye on my character.

Character means, "honor, nature, atmosphere, charisma, integrity, standing, and reputation," among other things. I have trained myself to know when I get annoyed and frustrated. This is where I have to consciously make a choice to either continue annoyed and lash out with words, or pull myself together and refuse to engage a foul spirit that can cause strife and dissension.

It takes more courage to compose oneself than to join an evil spirit. You may have never looked at it this way, but the Bible says, "Our struggle [or warfare] is not against flesh and blood…" (Eph. 6:12,

NIV). It is not people who initiate strife and arguments. The root causes are evil spirits that always try to inundate our atmosphere and upset our peace. Obedience to God's Word is the key that keeps the enemy at bay—unable to trespass. We must be aware of Satan's devices.

I have learned to be soft-spoken. "Soft speech breaks down the most bonelike resistance" (Prov. 25:15, AMP).

I refuse to add wood to a wild fire during an altercation. "As coals are to hot embers and as wood to fire, so is a quarrelsome man to inflame strife" (Prov. 26:21, AMP).

I am confident, never temperamental, moody, sulky, or unpredictable. "And you shall be secure and feel confident because there is hope; yes, you shall search about you, and you shall take your rest in safety" (Job 11:18, AMP).

I am open-minded about new things, new ideas, and especially change.

I do not over-talk. I always make sure that I abbreviate stories and never go on and on about something. "A quarrelsome wife is like a constant dripping on a rainy day" (Prov. 27:15, NIV).

I have learned never to lie, not even a white lie (as the old saying goes). Lying to cover up a mistake or to defend one of your children will eventually come to the light and cause heartache and great strife. Not only is lying a sin, but not lying is also one of the Ten Commandments given to us by God, which we are instructed to obey.

Developing a good character is learned. You are not born with it. Forming a habit of learning God's Word and demonstrating His attributes will instill in you remarkable character. "Many daughters have done virtuously, nobly, and well [with the strength of character that is steadfast in goodness], but you excel them all" (Prov. 31:29, AMP).

Dealing with illness (disease, sickness, ailments, virus, affliction)

Although I am enjoying forty-one good years of marriage, I have also been actively contending with a debilitating disease for seventeen years—a disease without a medical cure and for which I am taking medication. Many times I have felt the urge of giving up, retiring from ministry and writing, and leading a passive life. In retrospect I can see how the enemy would have loved for me to give up, become bitter, and adapt myself to a life of complaining and instability.

Instead I have chosen to believe and apply God's Word to my mind and body. My daily practice includes thanking God for healing, declaring that I am healed by faith even though I do not see a complete manifestation. My quest for healing has taken me to many physicians and different therapies. Pain in my body has become a frequent unwelcome companion, which I put under subjection with prayer and confession every night and morning. Do I complain, mumble, and grumble all the time? Please ask my husband and my daughters. They will tell you that I barely ever complain. They know I'm hurting when they see me reach for the pain medication. I have tremendous peace and know that Jesus is the healer whether I receive my total healing or not. My life has become an open testimony to many people of God's sustaining power.

When I get in front of an audience to speak, the Holy Spirit sustains me and enables me to deliver without pain or discomfort. I feel energized. I travel all the time, sometimes across continents, and God has been faithful to me. I remember a few weeks ago dashing as quickly as I could from one terminal to the other in the airport to make a connection. At first I thought I would succumb from the pain and not be able to make it on time, but as I hopped from one moving belt to the next I started confessing a scripture over and over: "I can do all things through Christ who strengthens me" (Phil. 4:13). I was exhilarated and flushed when I arrived at the gate without one bit of pain in my body. The supernatural power of God's Word just took over as I confessed and believed that I could run and leap and not be wearied or consumed. "For by You I can run against a troop, by my God I can leap over a wall" (Ps. 18:29).

Why am I being so transparent about so many things in my personal life? I believe it's the most effective way I can make you understand that God is real and His Word is alive and active, and that you too can have a wonderful, powerful marriage and undo the plans and strategies of your enemies. Jesus used parables to get a point across. I use real testimonies and life experiences.

This practice of believing God and confessing His Word over difficult situations has kept my marriage strong and stable. Whenever a problem arises in our family or business, I immediately say a specific powerful prayer and search for a scripture to confess as I believe God for an answer. Keeping my joy pumped up is a personal secret that I practice since I found this scripture a few years ago: "A *happy heart* is good medicine and a cheerful mind works healing, but a broken spirit dries up the bones" (Prov. 17:22, AMP, emphasis added).

Keeping your joy in the midst of trials and illness is good spiritual medicine that transmits into all your living cells. Maintaining a cheerful and optimistic mind works healing. What a truth this is! Every morning I get up with a song in my mind. Usually it's the praise and worship chorus taken from Psalm 100:4: "Enter into His gates with thanksgiving, and into His courts with praise." No matter how tough your situation may be, your invasion of praise into the atmosphere will scatter your enemies.

All of us are constantly faced with a challenge or problem of some kind. *What we do and how we act during times of adversity will determine the outcome of the situation.* I choose to confess and appropriate God's Word instead of allowing fear to dominate my senses. The foul spirits of fear and torment are not allowed into my atmosphere.

Now I want you to pay close attention to this advice. Read this paragraph several times and absorb the counsel. *If you learn to trust God in the midst of the storms and unexpected trials that will come your way, you will partake of one victory after another.* I am a witness.

If you choose to wail and beg God for help, fearing that your world is falling apart, you will not receive anything from God. The Word says: "The earnest (heartfelt, continued) prayer of a righteous man makes tremendous power available [dynamic in its working]" (James 5:16, AMP).

It also says: "I have given you authority and power to trample upon serpents and scorpions, and [physical and mental strength and ability] over all the power that the enemy [possesses]; and nothing shall in any way harm you" (Luke 10:19, AMP).

When sickness invades your body or the body of your spouse or children, immediately seek to do all the possible things that you can do. God will do the impossible things you can't do. Pray and ask God for wisdom. Thank Him for healing. Have your spouse lay hands on you and anoint with oil the affected area of sickness. Declare God's Word by confessing scriptures. Unite with a friend in a prayer of agreement. If necessary, go to a physician and follow his advice.

My favorite healing scripture is Proverbs 4:20–22. I quote this scripture every day. It's like taking medicine, and for seventeen years God continues to strengthen me.

> My *[daughter Iris]*, attend to my words; consent and submit to my sayings. Let them not depart from your sight; keep them in the center of your heart. For they are life to those who find them, healing and health to all their flesh.
>
> —PROVERBS 4:20–22, AMP

STRENGTHENING YOUR RELATIONSHIP WITH YOUR MATE

I look for something to admire every day.

To *admire* is to "esteem, respect, appreciate, regard, and approve." Men especially thrive on admiration. Here are some examples of things I habitually say:

- "Honey, I admire you for working so hard to support our family."

- "I admire your handiwork around the house."

- "Thanks for fixing the door; I can depend on you."

- "I admire you for going to church even when you're bone tired."

- "I admire your tenacity to get your work done."

- "I admire your courage for saying no to temptations."

- "Thanks for making coffee; I appreciate it."

- "Thanks for taking me out to dinner; it was really good."

- "I was proud of you today; you did a great job."

- "I admire you for helping me cook dinner."

When I admire my husband, it becomes natural for him to also admire me. Find something to appreciate, even if you don't feel like it.

Don't tolerate negative feelings. Instead, ask God to help you develop a positive attitude. Ask God to give you confidence to encourage and admire your spouse. After a while of purposefully looking for something to admire in your spouse, you will create a tremendous habit toward a powerful marriage.

Don't just get angry because your husband doesn't help out around the house. You can use your woman's ingenuity to sweetly request help. Some men don't help because they are not asked. They were reared accustomed to seeing Mom do everything.

Start admiring something, and enjoy the payback.

Frequent endearments (compliments, flattery, affection, sweet talk)

Saying "I love you" in our relationship is spontaneous, and many times deliberate and purposeful. The more you say something, the more you believe it. We both had to learn and practice this habit. We didn't learn this at a young age when life was racing by with dysfunction, too many demanding siblings, and exhausted parents. Experiencing abuse of any kind can also inhibit a person from spontaneously saying, "I love you dearly, and I care about you."

My knowledge of this practice came from the many books I read about marriage, parenting, and healing. Now it is second nature for us to look at each other and say, "I love you." Many times my husband will be engrossed in work, tired, and a little anxious. I'll sneak up to him purposefully, give him a kiss on his forehead, and say, "I love you. Thank you for working so hard. Can I help you or get you some coffee?" I notice how during these times, he exhales and calms down.

An endearment is an act of affection, a compliment, a kind and loving word, and flattery. Make it a practice in your marital relationship. It will smooth out a lot of rough edges. It will cause tenderness to surface.

Saying I love you and forgiving each other without holding grudges are very powerful ways of doing spiritual warfare. Without saying it, you are declaring, "Satan, you can't have my marriage!" The enemy of your soul desires that you be constantly involved in contentions.

In my family we say "I love you" so much that when the grandsons come in, they instantly say, "Papa, I love you, and Nana, I love you." Loving is contagious.

Respecting and honoring my husband

Respect means, "detail, value, appreciation, esteem, reverence, thoughtfulness, high opinion and regard." *Honor* means, "dignity of position, reputation, mark of distinction, personal integrity, great privilege, esteem, keep, award, revere, and source of pride." Ask a young married woman what honor means, and most of the time she will say *respect*. But even the word *respect* is just a word that sounds important to many couples and not something that God expects us to pay attention to and practice. Here are some of the simple ways I respect and honor my husband:

- I never share our marital problems with friends and never talk ill of him.

- I never correct him in public, even when I think he's wrong.

- When he's low, I lift him up with good words.

- When he's very tired, I never ask him to do anything. I try to get him to rest. This has worked so well that when I'm very tired, he makes me drop everything and go take a nap.

- I never criticize him or bring up negative things of the past.

- I never gossip to him about anyone.

- I never complain or raise my voice in anger or pout.

- We never go to bed angry (Eph. 4:26).

- I bless him and cover his faults (Gal. 6:2, AMP).

- I never make fun of him.

- We have developed a habit of saying "I'm sorry" when we offend each other.

- I never interrupt him when he's talking.

- I honor his position as head of our home (1 Cor. 11:3).

This next point is very crucial: I never chastise him with words when he has offended me or one of the children. Instead I go to my Abba Father and say, "Father God, Your son John has offended me. I am not his mother to chastise him, so please take care of him. I place him in Your hands." God always answers my prayer.

> He who covers and forgives an offense seeks love, but he who repeats or harps on a matter separates even close friends.
> —PROVERBS 17:9, AMP

Respecting and honoring my husband doesn't mean I have to agree with everything he says. We both have many different opinions about a lot of things. The important thing is that we respect each other's opinion without getting into arguments and bitter discussions. It also means that many times we'll agree without making a face, even though we differ in opinion. You'll be surprised how many times your spouse is right about the issue and you are wrong.

> When they observe the pure and modest way in which you conduct yourselves, together with your reverence [for your husband; you are to feel for him all that reverence includes: to respect, defer to, revere him—to honor, esteem, appreciate, prize, and, in the human sense, to adore him, that is, to admire, praise, be devoted to, deeply love, and enjoy your husband].
> —1 PETER 3:2, AMP

I pray and bless my husband every day.

Prayer is communication with God. In prayer you have a direct spiritual line of conversation. Powerful prayer is not about repetitious and memorized phrases.

The thesaurus describes prayer as: "to address, request, ask, hope strongly, implore, and meditate." The practice of prayer will instill respect for God—a respect that will spill over into all your relationships, especially your marriage.

I pray specifically and speak blessings such as these: "I bless my husband's mind today." "I decree that no weapon formed against him today will prosper." "Abba Father, I thank You for keeping him from all temptations and protecting him from all harm." "Close all doors of interruptions today, and open the doors of blessing." "I cover him with the blood of Jesus." My husband does the same for me. He prays specifically for me. We don't pray together as a couple all the time, but when I'm down, I always ask him to pray and rebuke the enemy. Not only is prayer very effective, but also the act of depending on each other for prayer has a bonding effect.

This is what spiritual warfare is all about. It's not looking for a demon in all the corners, but it's loving with faith. We are facing a war every day. The enemy of our souls, Satan, desires to steal our faith. He couldn't care less if we read and memorize the whole Bible, go to church every week, and help the poor. If the enemy can discourage and prevent you from praying and believing God, he has you conquered. Discouragement, as well as lack of prayer and joy, will eventually devastate your belief system and your marriage.

When my husband is annoyed or disturbed for whatever reason, I lift him up to God in prayer as I use my keys of binding and loosing, commanding all attacks of the enemy to go from him in the name of Jesus (Matt. 16:19). I also loose the peace of God into his heart. Prayer is powerful. The enemy has to obey the commands of a child of God who is walking in obedience.

An example of one of the specific prayers I might pray is:

Father God, I thank You for helping my husband today, guiding his steps, and keeping him from temptation. I thank You for closing all doors of interruption and waste of time. Protect his mind and give him creative ideas. Guard his heart from all evil and from the attacks of the enemy.

Continuous wooing

I love this statement by C. M. Ward in his little booklet *Husbands and Wives* written in 1976:

> The man who can make a woman feel more happy to be a woman is truly a man indeed. He does not have to go around beating his chest to show how masculine he is. Such continuous courtship is based on the great spiritual truth. "He that loseth his life…shall find it" (Matthew 10:39 [kjv]).
>
> If you are going to love your wife, sir, you are at least going to have to love some of the things she loves: her children, her home, her flowers, her favorite dishes, her vacation choice, her mother, her hobby, her taste in reading, her music, her church, and her God! Love isn't just a ten-minute occasional hug-and-wrestling-match. Love must compass mind, soul, spirit, and body.[1]

Don't you just love this? My husband and I practice continuous wooing. We still date, go occasionally to the movies, enjoy candle-light dinners, give each other a massage, whisper little secrets, and cuddle together while watching TV. He still opens the door and pulls out the chair for me everywhere we go. He buys me flowers, and I occasionally buy him his favorite cherry Danish and cream soda. I still fold a little love note in his underwear while I pack his luggage before he leaves on a long trip. We still text each other romantic quips and endearments. You say, "Oh, that is so old-fashioned." Sadly, that is also what a lot of people are saying about being a Christian who radically believes in obeying the Ten Commandments.

We have gotten so far away from what is good and romantic—the things that truly make a marriage flourish and grow strong, that many young couples have no clue how to court each other and have a wonderful, powerful marriage. They think that sitting in front of a TV and enjoying their popcorn and pizza while they Facebook and text their friends is the new kind of spending quality time together. Like my pastor says, "Call me a taxi!" Same thing goes for many young people attending church services—they want to be entertained. They sit back like spectators, never learning how to really enter into God's presence and come out of that service feeling energized and transformed by God's Word. Ah, what a great need there is for training among our young couples and those soon to be married. Christian headlines have been reporting that there is a great interest among this generation to really know God and be radical in their faith. I truly hope this new hunger will take deep roots that will affect our next generations. We need a change. Too many marriages are ending up in divorce for trivial reasons.

Brother Ward also says:

> Happiness does not come automatically. It is a by-product of the successful accomplishments of many tasks and the development of many skills. It is the dividend for doing the right thing at the right time in the right way with the right motive. It is the overwhelming desire and persistent effort of two people to create for each other conditions under which each can become the person God meant him and her to be. And in this work, man is to take and maintain the lead! That is what the New Testament says, mister.[2]

I hope we can all follow this strong advice from this caring man of God. I just thought of a scripture that kind of fits in with this advice: "All the days of the afflicted are evil, but he who is of a merry heart has a *continual feast*" (Prov. 15:15, emphasis added).

Go ahead and learn how to have a continuous feast with your honey and your family!

We educate each other.

Educate means to "teach, instruct, edify, tutor, train, coach, inform, and develop." Every time I read or hear about something important, new, or evolving, I share it with my husband. This may sound strange to you, but I also inform him of new trends and help him with his research for new teaching material. We educate each other about better ways of ministering to people's needs. We also correct each other when we slip or say the wrong thing.

I love to read and mark all over my books. I even write key words and the page number on the blank page at the end of the book for future reference. One of my habits that my husband enjoys is when I read the highlights I have marked from an interesting book or document. I usually do this during a long drive. Men per se do not enjoy lots of details, and this allows them to get the meat of the story.

Another important area is letting each other know our personal needs. If your partner doesn't know your needs, he can't meet them. Educating each other will create a deeper understanding of each other's needs as well as better communication. This process has been one of our defining strengths.

Just recently I asked him to please protect my time from outside interruptions so that I could write this book. We both work out of our home offices. He has been considerate by providing someone to answer phones, provide meals, and attend to visitors.

This process of educating and edifying each other has to be a team effort. You may be dreaming of taking a sabbatical from work or enrolling in a community college class or having another baby.

Convey your desires to each other and create a plan. Set a goal, and keep it. You will enjoy life a lot more.

A few years ago I took notes of one of Jack Hayford's televised teachings on marriage, and he said, "Women, love in such a way as to grow a man. Men, love to grow a woman. Women, follow divine order." To *grow* means to "develop, expand, increase, cultivate, nurture, and become greater," and I will add to this, *to educate*.

Women, it is our duty to be a helpmate to our husbands and to help them to mature and become great men of God. As an added reward, your marital life will flow with God's blessings when you follow the divine order established in God's Word. Husband, it is your duty to grow your wife and help her mature, increase, and become a wonderful woman of God.

We keep each other healthy and well groomed.

Healthy means, "fit, functioning well, strong, vigorous, and good physical shape." *Groomed* means, "turned-out, dressed, presented, cleaned, spruced, and prepared."

Ah, some of you may wince and say, "Here we go again with the diet thing." Please read carefully, and listen to a voice of experience. Did I say this was a mentoring book? Yes, I did. This spiritual mother wants you to *get it*!

Hippocrates, the father of modern medicine, said: "All disease begins in the gut." I strive not only to prepare healthy meals, but also to administer vitamins and supplements and to supervise the well-being of my husband. When I realized that this was a tedious and sacrificial endeavor, I reasoned with myself that either I pay now or pay later. With the years I have mastered the habit of consistency and a good disposition, and we are reaping the benefits.

Looking good, feeling good, and smelling good are areas of utmost importance in a marriage. You may think, "Oh, well, if he doesn't like the way I look, too bad!" I've heard this statement many times. It just doesn't work like that. Our attitude will affect everything we do. Satan is always looking for a bad attitude, a sluggish body, and a careless disposition so that he can inflict his torment.

If you become careless, somewhere along your marital journey you will drop seeds of carelessness and disorder. When the seeds spring up, and they will, you'll find they have multiplied and many times morphed into other characteristics, such as a critical spirit. The sad thing about this scenario is that a husband and wife are role models who are always planting seeds into their garden and into their children, whether they want to or not.

There's a psychological ambiance that takes place when we get up in the morning and, like the Bible says, anoint ourselves, present our day to God in prayer, and get ourselves groomed and ready to face the world. Everything snaps into place. We feel put together. Every day I get compliments from my husband on my appearance. Jewelry enhances any woman. I love to wear it, even if I'm dressed in jeans and a T-shirt. It doesn't have to be expensive, just appealing.

> Therefore wash yourself and anoint yourself, put on your best garment...
>
> —RUTH 3:3

Imagine the opposite scenario of getting up blurry-eyed, in a bad mood, tending to kids, preparing an instant breakfast, running off to work, huffing and puffing, and putting on makeup while you drive. I'm tired already thinking of this scenario.

By going through many unpleasant situations during the first years of my marriage, I have learned to discipline myself to do the things that bring orderliness to my world. It took persistent practice. Today I'm sharing this information with you in the hope that you grasp the importance of looking and feeling good before your life becomes undone.

First thing in the morning, I do my hygiene, put on my makeup, fix my hair, walk into my closet, dress, and then make coffee. I now look good enough to receive any visitor. All this before my husband gets up, which is about an hour before he usually starts his day. With my coffee in hand, I go to my private office and render my sacrifice of thanksgiving, praise, and joy. Now I'm ready to roll. By this time, almost an hour later, my husband is ready for breakfast. Is this a habit? Yes, it is!

These are habits you should develop early on in your marriage. When the kids come along, you work around them and develop a system that works, whether it is getting up earlier or getting ready right after they go to school. All households are different, but when you purposefully implement a plan of action, you will notice that your home will run like a well-oiled engine.

I also like to keep healthy snacks, such as nuts and dried fruit that provide natural energy, on the kitchen counter in see-through containers, as well as a supply of flavored water and fresh fruit. The objective is to do all the little things that show thoughtfulness and caring love, but also to provide enjoyment.

In-law interference

Personally, I have never had problems with my in-laws. From the beginning of our marriage my husband put his foot down and informed his dad that he was the boss in his home. Good for him and for me! His mom was a gem. My mom was another gem—never meddled in anything. Yet, while this was my situation, I know from counseling many couples that many in-laws are known for wrecking and intruding in their children's marriages.

The Bible says: "Therefore a man shall leave his father and his mother and shall become united and *cleave* to his wife, and they shall become one flesh" (Gen. 2:24, AMP, emphasis added). To *cleave* means, "to leave, to stick, penetrate, cut, and to cling faithfully." The

Bible gives married couples this specific instruction of leaving and cleaving to each other because it is extremely important.

In-laws who try to control their children's marriage do so in disobedience to God's written Word. God knew from the beginning that a couple needed to faithfully cleave together without the interference of parents. As parents, we are to be good role models, always praying and loving our children unconditionally. It is our duty as Christian parents to always be ready to give counsel and help when requested from our children, not whenever we feel it is appropriate.

In-law control and manipulation: I've been confronted by many a dominant and controlling mother, asking me to intervene on her behalf for a son or daughter having marital problems. It never fails that the mothers become angry with me when I suggest they keep their hands off the situation. A controlling and manipulative mother- or father-in-law, always interjecting and imposing their views, likes, and dislikes in their child's marital relationship, is like a demonic force that eventually will explode. Many couples choose to live far away from their families just to avoid a nagging and controlling in-law.

Control and manipulation are foul spirits that steal the joy out of any relationship. You would be amazed at the incredible number of young married couples who have relational issues with their in-laws. Not only do these issues separate families, but when grandchildren come along, there is no enjoyment and bonding. Many young women are desperate to have a loving and relaxed friendship with their own mother, but because of the control issue, they are separated and devastated.

This counsel is for all young couples—leave and cleave! Don't bad-mouth, criticize, make faces, or gossip. The Bible is your instruction manual to guide you to possess a dynamic and pleasure-filled marriage and family. In-laws should be a healthy extension of your marriage, not an unlawful intrusion.

If you're an in-law experiencing or causing strife in your children's marriage, try backing off and just loving your children. Don't give any advice unless they ask you for it. Be gentle, kind, and a prayer warrior. Your prayers will do much more than your intervention. Love your grandchildren, and never criticize or correct them in front of their parents. And please, don't mention weight issues or try to show how to budget finances, cook, keep house, and raise the children.

Control and manipulation are spirits that affect many people. They go hand in hand with rebellion, which is labeled as a sin of witchcraft in the Bible. It is also referred to as a Jezebel spirit.

> For rebellion is as the sin of witchcraft, and stubbornness is as idolatry.
>
> —1 SAMUEL 15:23, AMP

A person operating under this spirit may not realize he is doing anything wrong. Strife and arguments are indications that this spirit may be at work in your family. When a woman does all the talking, and her husband can barely get a word in, or when she makes all the decisions whether he likes it or not, watch out for this spirit in action. Prayer and renunciation will be necessary to oust this spirit. Get a powerful prayer partner and decide to be free. This advice will heap up rewards for you. In your old age, you will have children who will care for you without griping. Many lonely in-laws in nursing homes today wish they had heeded this advice.

I found it necessary to add this advice, even though I myself do not have in-law problems. But so many couples are affected and broken up over in-law control that teaching on this subject is absolutely essential.

CREATING A PLEASANT HOME ENVIRONMENT

Home-cooked meals and eating out

Eating at the kitchen table with your spouse is a pleasing habit that has to be formed and cultivated. It doesn't just happen. Today most families eat at different times and in front of the television. This practice of cooking at home and setting the table will be one of the most rewarding habits you and your spouse, and later your family, will enjoy. I like to prep everything the night before, such as cleaning the lettuce, marinating the meat, and chopping vegetables. Many times I prepare two meals at once, such as a baked pasta dish or a stew. I recommend you use your nice plates and glasses. Save the paper stuff for parties. Invest a couple of dollars for a few fresh flowers, and put them in a small vase for a touch of romance and beauty. Decorate with seasonal colorful place mats. Making this a habit is actually easier than you may think.

This practice is something I do consistently, and now my grown daughters imitate me. When they invite me to dinner at their home, I notice all the same fine touches I use at my own table. Children will always imitate everything you do. Enjoy God's goodness while you're young. Don't wait until someone has to help you out because you no longer have the energy.

I prepare a menu every Saturday and do all grocery shopping at one time for the week. I try to pay attention to our weight and adjust the menus accordingly. Preparing balanced and nutritious meals is so important that I recommend you make this a very important priority. We try to avoid bad carbohydrates and eat the good carbs from vegetables, fruits, and whole wheat. I cook almost everything with olive oil. Many years ago I stopped eating pork and its by-products after doing research on this animal. The Bible also says it is unclean, and that's good enough for me. Staying healthy and fit is part of the discipline and self-control necessary for great marriages.

Eating out has become a modern-day phenomenon. Many young couples come into a marriage accustomed to eating out with their families and while they were dating. It becomes a burden for them to prepare a meal at home. Even more alarming is the fact that most young women do not learn how to cook. They enter marriage totally unprepared for the assignment.

The problem with all this eating out is that it is expensive and fattening! Many couples cannot afford to eat out, but they do it anyway. When *misery* knocks on their door, they become helpless. After a while, all the excuses in the world will not fix the problem or get a person out of debt. The only solution here is coming up with a serious plan and sticking with it—whether it is digging out the cooking books and following a recipe or getting together with a group of friends from church and creating some cooking classes. That sounds like fun! The objective is to start somewhere. Make the effort.

Now that I'm older and my nest is empty, I take more time to teach my daughters how to cook, and sometimes they teach me new recipes. I have even invited a group of single women to my home and taught them how to cook different stir-fry dishes by demonstrating step by step how it's done for two people. Then I take out of the oven a large skillet of the same recipe, ready to eat. It's a blast and they love it, while at the same time they learn how to cook several different dishes with the same technique. I recommend this advice to those of you who love to cook. Invite a group of young women to your home and teach them how to cook. It will bless their marriages.

Take my advice and cook at home as much as you can. It is very rewarding and healthy. Most of the portions served in restaurants are very large. In fact, you can easily serve two people with one portion. This is where the fattening part comes in. God has given us wisdom to make wise decisions. Cooking at home is a wonderful part of creating a powerful marriage.

Care of clothing, laundry, cleaners

This thing about doing laundry and ironing became a huge issue when I first got married. My husband was used to the way his mother did things: socks rolled up like sausages and neatly stacked, T-shirts folded perfectly, shirts ironed with medium starch and on hangers, jeans stiffly starched and pleated, and suits taken to the cleaners every other week. "Wow, what a load of work," I thought. My mom had nine kids and no time to iron. She just shook the stuff out on the clothesline, and unless it was Sunday, we wore it *aired out*.

Needless to say, a confrontation ensued almost immediately when out came his socks from the dryer and into a hamper until I had time to sort them out, which sometimes I forgot. Arguments got louder and louder as things were just not the same as his mother did them. A year later I realized that if I didn't make an effort to make some changes and adjustments, I would be involved in continual day-and-night arguments.

I made the effort. Most of his stuff went to the cleaners. His socks got rolled up like sausages, and his T-shirts were folded neatly. Peace on earth! Forty-one years later and all is well—my housekeeper does the socks and T-shirts. Now what am I trying to teach you here?

- Learn to have a system that works. Find out how your spouse likes to have his clothes groomed, and make the effort to please him. You will avoid a ton of headaches.

- Train yourself to do the laundry at least twice a week, and quickly get it out of the dryer and unto hangers or folded.

- Create good habits, and you'll have great results.

Why is this subject important? Because this issue is a big deal!

Keeping the house clean

Keeping a clean house tells a lot about a person's character and personality. Some of us were taught as young girls or boys to do chores and keep the room always clean. Some children are never taught these important tasks because someone else always does them.

The advantage of teaching your children responsibility for their own messes is immensely important. Even if children have a nanny or housekeeper, it is important that they learn to clean up after themselves. In general, young married couples are not able to afford a housekeeper and, even less, a nanny to keep their children.

I remember having to help my mother clean house every weekend. Sometimes I was not in the mood to clean. My mind was somewhere else. One particular Saturday I decided to hurry, so I kicked most of the dirty clothes under the bed. Two days later my mother discovered the dirty clothes, and I had to spend hours paying for my bad deed, but I learned a valuable lesson.

Keeping a home clean is necessary for the well-being of the entire family. *An orderly room conveys discipline and attention and is conducive to relaxation and peace.* Entering a home where clothes, shoes, and dirty dishes lay all over the place is like entering a war zone. A person cannot concentrate or feel at ease or even invite a visitor.

Disorganization is a characteristic that runs through every fiber of a person's being. It is also a trait that can be changed and transformed. Many children are reared in very disorganized homes, and they often bring the same customs into their own homes.

Part of the success in my own marriage is an orderly, clean, and good-smelling home to live in and welcome friends and family every day. Yes, I do work at least forty hours a week, and I do make time for my grandsons and cook at least three days a week. But I also make it my business to keep a clean and orderly home.

If you are a stay-at-home mom, your home should be wonderfully inviting, even if you have several children. If you work more than forty hours and have children, you must learn to enlist everyone's help by assigning chores and sticking to a schedule. Some of you can afford a housekeeper one day a week if you cut back on some trivial things. The important point I'm trying to make is that it is possible and very important to have an orderly and inviting home. My thoughts are candid. Some may hurt, but, just like surgery, it must hurt before it gets better.

Discipline is the key here. My home is so inviting that my husband has a hard time accepting invitations to eat out, and my grandsons want to spend all their weekends in our home. Does it take work and effort—absolutely!

Making and keeping appointments

I keep a yearly detailed calendar of all appointments. I make sure that I schedule medical checkups and dental appointments as recommended by the physicians. It is never a question of *should we* but *when* is my next dental appointment. This discipline takes action and reaps many benefits. We also keep ministry appointments on a desk calendar and in our cell phones. Being on time to an appointment is as important as keeping an appointment.

Forming good habits from the beginning will strengthen your marriage in all areas. Great habits create great achievers. Keeping and making appointments will reinforce other good habits. *Forgetting appointments and frequently being late will cause strife and arguments in any marriage.* Many times, lack of success can be attributed to lack of consistency and orderliness.

Shopping habits

Unsupervised and unplanned shopping habits will cause chaos in any marriage. This is one of the hot buttons that causes too many couples to end up in strife and arguments. Constant arguments over spending habits will undermine and make a marital relationship very unstable.

In my home, shopping for something is everybody's business, not a spontaneous activity. When one of us needs a pair of shoes or a new outfit, the request is made to each other. My husband and I are accountable to each other. Once we determine if there is money available and the purchase is really necessary, we proceed to make the purchase. Same thing goes with anything else. So many of us have cramped drawers, closets, and garages full of expensive unnecessary things stored away, sometimes for years. It's like an epidemic. We really need to make an assessment of our shopping habits and ask God to forgive us.

Learn to make a list of the things needed, whether it's groceries, clothing, shoes, or medications. A list will always help determine what is important or urgent and what is not. Keep the list in your purse and be ready to refer to it when a big sale comes along and you happen to be ready to make the purchase.

I've met several manic-depressive people who feel like they have to shop every day. My advice: get help! I remember praying for a dear friend with this problem. Her home was in chaos. After professional counsel and several prayers of deliverance from demonic oppression, she was set free. You may cringe at this information, but I've seen it with my own eyes.

To declare and believe the statement "Satan, you can't have my marriage!", we first must deal with all the inconsistencies that rob our substance, our joy, and, in many instances, our very life. *For a marriage to be blessed and healthy, we must learn to do things the right way.* Make learning all you can about how to have a wonderful marriage a priority as soon as possible before your marriage ends up as another casualty.

This counsel is not only for young couples. There are many married couples out there just barely hanging on by a thread—disgusted, frustrated, unhappy, barren, in poverty, and feeling abandoned and stuck. They can't even smell the blessings.

It is time to set yourself free from all curses and come to Jesus, your Savior. Get help! Make some drastic changes! Go to a discipleship class in a good Bible-believing church, and get some training. Read some good books, like this one. Read it over and over until you understand the conflict we're in between good and evil!

ENJOYING AND TRAINING YOUR CHILDREN

Establishing boundaries and priorities

My husband and I have clear and specific boundaries. No child, ministry, employer, culture, or trend will interfere or make us compromise our belief system and our boundaries.

In our home we protect our values and priorities. God is first, spouse second, and children and vocation follow right behind. Our modern Christian family is rapidly adapting the world's system from God's intended purpose for marriage. Work, work, and more work is taking priority over God, spouse, and family. Babysitters or relatives are increasingly taking care of our children.

Couples need to negotiate ways of doing things that will fit their lifestyles and belief systems. Opposing views between the parents and the children—such as Christian versus non-Christian, traditional versus conservative, even Republican versus Democrat—can stir contentions. Young couples living too close or in the same house with parents need to develop boundaries that will create mutual respect.

Here are some practical suggestions besides leaving and cleaving:

- Respect and honor your parents but live independently of them, in separate homes if at all possible.

- Under all circumstances, put your mate first. It's good to help your mom and dad in a time of need, but recognize that your spouse and children are your number one priority.

- Remember that your children are your number one obligation. Do not assume your parents are your number one babysitters. Always plan ahead.

- Be vigilant and guard the boundaries of all visitors, housekeepers, babysitters, or a live-in relative. Don't allow them freedom to become too friendly or spend too much time alone with your spouse. The enemy will take advantage of every opportunity to inflict temptation and cause your mate to fall. I've seen too many couples divorce because too many boundaries were broken and too many doors kept open for temptation to come in.

Neglect in these areas will always produce regrets.

Home entertainment (amusement, attraction, enjoyment, performance)

We never watch pornographic or sexually explicit material, movies, or shows. Do you realize that allowing young children to watch pornographic and sexually explicit movies or videos is a form of child abuse? Many young children's minds have been raped (violated by forced, violent destructive treatment) while sitting in front of a TV or movie screen. I personally know children who were exposed to movies with gross, filthy, and repulsive sexual content at a very tender young age by trusted relatives. Now you can understand why I can write with such candidness. Many children develop insecurity problems at a tender age. For some of them, it may be many years later when they are able to confess their secretive experiences. In their hearts they knew what they were watching was wrong, but because a trusted relative or friend was involved and sanctioned the behavior, they didn't dare tell.

All traumatic experiences during childhood will produce negative effects in the person. Many people never learn to recover. Children will grow into adults with insecurities that may take years to unravel. When healthy conflict-management skills are not modeled in the family of origin, a person may forever be a victim of his past, unless he has an encounter with the redeeming and transforming love of God.

A parent may never see the actual damaging effects caused in the child's mind, but something has radically changed forever as a result of abuse. Many children exposed to graphic sexual content become promiscuous at an early age. Some develop habits of masturbation, insecurity, and low self-esteem. If you're a young couple with children or are planning to have children, please take this counsel seriously.

The following is an important excerpt on this subject from my book *Satan, You Can't Have My Children*. I recommend that you read this together as a couple and carefully do everything in your power to be alert and vigilant and committed to making your home a safe haven for each other and your family.

> Many wife abusers will tell you that their father abused their mother. Many prostitutes will tell you that some family member sexually abused them. Many unfaithful wives will tell you that their father abused them. Many fathers who cannot get along with their daughters or sons will tell you that they did not have a good relationship with their father or mother. Many husbands who do not respect their wives will tell you that their father did not respect their mother. Many homosexual men will tell you that they were molested by a family member or another man when they were very young. The cycle continues, and it is very vicious.
>
> Lust and pornography will destroy marriages and relationships. The root has to be destroyed, and the person's mind has to be renewed by the Word of God and by fellowship with the Holy Spirit. These sins are never committed alone. Satan is always a participant, and your children and their children are the inheritors of the same sin or sins.[3]

A child is affected not only by what he sees and hears but also by what surrounds him. Parents may think they are watching X-rated movies in a private room away from the children, but these same X-rated spirits will affect the behavior and sleep patterns of the children. They don't even have to be in the same room.[4]

Protecting your home from the effects of pornographic content should be top priority. My husband and I enjoy watching sports, news, and selected movies, but we seriously protect our atmosphere. Sometimes I prepare popcorn and soda floats. Many times we'll call the grandkids over and order pizza. We try to make the most of every opportunity to laugh and become silly for a little while. Our living room sometimes turns into a literal tent with blankets and pillows scattered everywhere. When you consider the short time we have to truly enjoy each other and train our children, it becomes an urgent responsibility to protect their spirits from as much garbage of this world as possible. We must set the example in our homes by prohibiting demonic influence. I always tell them, "Garbage in—garbage out."

Avoid perfectionism

Allowing your family to rumple up your family room may be a tough scene for some wives who want to see everything perfect. I believe trying to achieve perfectionism in a home environment will cause hostility and separation. We only have one life to live, and either we make it full of fun and good memories or full of regrets and loneliness. The thesaurus describes *perfectionism* as: "fastidiousness, fussiness, nitpicking, meticulousness, rigorousness, and demand for perfection." I've met several wives who fit this description, and they all had one thing in common: bitterness.

There are many men and women living in retirement facilities because their children cannot put up with their parents' nitpicky fastidiousness. Learn to enjoy life today, and tomorrow your family will enjoy life with you.

Beyond every person's facade is a desire to enjoy a happy home, have fun, and truly relax. But looking around, we see too many unhappy marriages. If we would learn to apply God's precepts of love, truth, and faith to everything we do, we would start enjoying each other and reaping benefits for eternity.

Believe me when I say I'm not mincing words here or trying to impress you. *Living by the principles of the Word of God is spiritual warfare.* You don't have to strive to have a good, vivacious, and healthy marriage. All you have to do is obey God's Word and learn to love and set priorities. Start educating your mind and practicing some of the things that have enriched my marriage. I had to learn all by myself after contending with an abusive father. It took me one step at a time. I wish someone had given me a book with the advice contained here.

Start planning fun activities. Learn to relax. Enjoy your spouse and your children. Have a consciousness of the spiritual presence of God in your life. Ask yourself, "Can God be invited into all my fun activities?"

Keeping traditions

I love traditions, and so does my family. My husband and my family love the aroma of turkey greeting them at the door on Thanksgiving Day. Once my mother-in-law passed away, I took over the role of cooking the Thanksgiving meal. I made it my business to learn how to prepare everything just like my mother and my mother-in-law, down to the gravy. With time, I have added my own special touches.

During the Christmas holidays we enjoy going to church together as a family to the candlelight celebration on Christmas Eve, followed by a special meal of roasted meats with all the delicious trimmings and home-baked pies in my home. I can feel the deep sighs from some of you who have never attempted a holiday meal. All it takes is knowledge, which is easily accessible online and in some of the cooking shows, and practice. If you're a young married wife, don't be bashful to ask for cooking lessons from your mom or mother-in-law. This is one of our wonderful traditions.

Celebrating birthdays, anniversaries, and special events creates expectancy and special bonding. These are occasions that your husband and children will always look forward to, even as they grow older. You'll look back at all the memories sealed in photographs forever.

Never underestimate the positive effect of keeping traditions. Of all the good things my family has enjoyed over the years, I would say that keeping traditions and enjoying the different festivities and celebrations together rate as number one.

Family problems and intervention

When our children have a problem, we privately discuss the matter first and together agree on proper intervention and counsel. We decide if a hands-off attitude and prayer are the wise thing to do or if we need to offer our help. We never lend money to our children or relatives without mutual consent, and never on the sneak.

If one of our daughters confides a secret to one of us, we protect the confidence. If we decide that both of us need to be involved, we first consult with our daughter about sharing the problem with us openly. This approach has created a deep bond of confidence and respect between us and our children.

There will always be a time when we must come face-to-face with problems relating to our children. As a couple, we must face these problems together and use wisdom and understanding to turn the problems into learning and growing experiences. For a deeper discussion on this subject, please read my book *Satan, You Can't Have My Children*, published by Charisma House.

Today we are confronted with the growing number of

irresponsible young adults who have not learned to keep their jobs or handle money. Perhaps you may be a parent going through hardships because of unstable children. As long as you keep providing the handouts and condoning irresponsible behavior, they will keep coming back for more. Change is possible. The truth is, parents are responsible for their children's behavior. Therefore, change must begin within the parent responsible for the unstable children. This advice is not easy to swallow.

As adults, we do not want to take responsibility for difficult children. In order for effective change to start taking place in a long-standing situation, counsel and retraining will have to take place. Seek help from your spiritual leader and a godly counselor. Start praying for God's wisdom and guidance to implement change in your home.

Spiritual warfare begins in the heart—with a desire to be rid of all demonic influence and interruptions. Pray powerful prayers that will break yokes. Remain steadfast in your decision to make positive changes. The Holy Spirit will help you every step of the way.

MAINTAINING EDIFYING
FELLOWSHIP WITH OTHERS

Entertaining friends in your home

To *entertain* means, "enjoy, amuse, accommodate, consider, humor, engage, compel." Entertaining guests is not a natural ability; it is learned and becomes easier with practice. Having friends over and serving food or dessert is a lot of fun. Married couples should not shy away from this practice just because they haven't done it before, feel inadequate, or don't have a beautiful home. A humble spirit and a humble attitude are attributes that God blesses and people love. When you engage people at their level and show humility, you'll have friends forever.

For some people it comes easily. They have the special gift of hospitality. For others it can become a nightmare. If you fall in the nightmare category, I recommend that you either enlist help or learn to start simply. By that I mean if your husband loves company but you feel unable to put a social party together, keep it simple by having everyone bring a dish or part of a meal, or order pizza and make a salad. Enroll your husband as your number one teammate. The main thing is to learn to lose the fear and learn to love people.

I prepare myself mentally and spiritually for events, guests, engagements, special holidays, and so forth. Preparation makes way for celebration and eliminates frustration. Not only do I ask God for strength and favor, but I also ask for creative ideas and patience. Any kind of event that involves serving people requires time, expense, and attention. To be a *good* host your mind has to be at ease, and you have to enjoy serving others. Entertaining friends and developing friendships take time and practice and become very rewarding.

Writing thank-you notes and correspondence

Not all men enjoy the task of sending a thank-you note for a special favor, meal, or gift. I enjoy keeping a good assortment of personalized stationary and thank-you cards. Saying "thank you" is an act of humility and appreciation. I almost always handwrite the thank-you cards for my husband and make sure he reads and approves them. I consider this part of being a good helpmate. Usually I do this the next day after the occasion.

I am also my husband's personal secretary and handle all his personal correspondence and filing. I like to do it in such a way that when I need to refer to an address or a specific document, it is easily accessible in a filing cabinet or a computer file.

"Hard work," you say? Yes, all good things demand effort and sacrifices. For something to be good, it has to cost you something. Does it pay off? Yes indeed. You will be remembered as someone who is exceptional and extraordinary.

Church attendance and fun activities

For us, going to church is not an option. Through the years I have mastered the habit of getting everything ready the night before. Sunday is our Sabbath, a sacred day dedicated to God. Our children never asked, "Are we going to church today?" Today they are grown and have kept the same custom. We meet at church on Sundays and enjoy lunch together afterward.

My husband and I thrive on spending time together just hanging out at least twice a month. We walk the mall, go to a fine restaurant, see a movie, go to a farmer's market, or drive out a couple of hours enjoying the sights, just because! Once a week we enjoy lunch together somewhere.

Once a month we invite a couple or two over for dinner. It doesn't have to be strenuous. Sometimes we order pizza, pick up a rotisserie chicken and make a salad, or put some steaks on the grill. Enjoying time together and creating good relationships with other married couples is fun and necessary. Cultivating good friendships will always assure you that you have someone to depend on and call for prayer when the need arises.

Some couples never socialize enough to develop deep ties with other Christians. After a while they find themselves alienated and bored. This is one of the reasons why faithful church attendance and involvement with other couples are so important. This practice is also extremely important for children to learn how to bond and, most importantly, to learn how to love God with all their hearts.

Through counseling many couples, I have discovered that one of the main reasons for failure is the lack of spiritual understanding. If a couple does not receive instruction and learn to apply the principles contained in the Bible to build a solid marriage foundation, it is inevitable that the couple will never know how to handle the difficulties and crises that will confront them. Not only is it good to attend church services on Sunday, but even more importantly, a young couple should make it their business to attend a midweek Bible class to receive valuable instruction. Feeding your spirit should become much more important than feeding your body.

In my book *Satan, You Can't Have My Children,* I dedicate a whole section to the importance of nurturing your child's spirit just as you would take care of a child's physical body. If you truly want to succeed in life and enjoy a powerful, blessed marriage, please take my advice and nourish each other's spirit on a daily basis.

CHAPTER EIGHT

IS SATAN ABUSE TROUBLING YOUR MARRIAGE?

Stop Satan from trespassing on your territory!

The thief does not come except to steal, and to kill, and to destroy. I have come that they might have life, and that they may have it more abundantly.

—JOHN 10:10

WE ALL KNOW about child abuse, spousal abuse, animal abuse, senior abuse, medical abuse, drug abuse, environmental abuse, religious abuse, terrorist abuse, government abuse, prison abuse, ritual abuse, and I'm sure you can think of many other forms of abuse.

The phrase *Satan-abuse* entered my mind during my prayer time this morning. "Wow," I thought, "the most pervasive kind of abuse is subtly and cleverly invading every facet of life." The statistics reveal that crisis is affecting and touching us from every corner of the universe. Abuse of every kind is prevalent and widespread. Every home on this earth is being invaded with the attacks, wiles, strategies, plans, and tactics of Satan and his evil workers of iniquity.

I truly hope that you pay attention to this and cast fear out of your heart as you read this. You may have a wonderful home, and this counsel may be for you to help someone else. Many Christians are fearful of even saying the word *Satan*. I was recently interviewed on a radio station, and I heard myself say, "A few years ago when the first edition of my book *Satan, You Can't Have My Children* first came out, I remember the fearful faces of many people when they picked up the book and saw the word *Satan* across the cover." But today, demonic content in almost every venue of entertainment is so rampant and out of control that beginning with our young people, it seems that even many Christians are becoming desensitized about who is the real enemy.

Today the name *Satan* is so pervasive and paid homage to in so much of today's entertainment, media, movies, music, religions, games, sitcoms, and dedicated websites that people are no longer amazed, awed, or afraid. They may not say they believe in and worship Satan, but their values and actions reveal that Jesus Christ is not their Lord. There is only God and Satan, good and evil. We serve one or the other, and not choosing is a choice! We can determine on what side a person is by their fruit.

> You will fully recognize them by their fruits.... Even so, every healthy (sound) tree bears good fruit [worthy of admiration], but the sickly (decaying, worthless) tree bears bad (worthless) fruit. A good (healthy) tree cannot bear bad (worthless) fruit, nor can a bad (diseased) tree bear excellent fruit [worthy of admiration]. Every tree that does not bear good fruit is cut down and cast into the fire. Therefore, you will fully know them by their fruits.
>
> —MATTHEW 7:16–20, AMP

Abuse means, "maltreatment, swearing, insult to somebody, improper use, improper practice, drug and alcohol misuse, misuse something, masturbate, exploitation, manipulation, mishandling, misapplication, and taking advantage."

THE EFFECTS OF ALCOHOL AND DRUG ABUSE IN A MARRIAGE

Volumes of information have been written about the devastating effect that substance abuse of alcohol and illegal drugs has had and is having on our society. The *Baker Encyclopedia of Psychology* states:

> A substance is defined as any chemical that modifies mood or behavior by affecting the central nervous system and whose use is subject to misuse. Such a definition obviously excludes the use of medications when they are used as prescribed. Pathological use of substances may include legal drugs (such as caffeine) or illegal drugs (such as cocaine). A substance-use disorder is characterized by maladaptive behavior associated with the use of substances.[1]

Too many homes are being devastated, broken, torn apart, and transformed into nightmares by a spouse who has allowed alcohol to control his or her life. Some men come into the marital relationship drinking just enough to keep them sober. Some only drink the occasional beer or wine, while others do have a serious problem with drinking hard liquor and many times passing out and becoming incoherent.

The phrase "love is blind" comes into play here when a young woman is blind enough not to see the danger signs for marrying a man who has a drinking or substance abuse problem.

During an interview I had with one abusive husband, he said, "My wife nagged me so much that I couldn't take it any more. I met some of my mates at the local pub, and we began to knock down a few. The more I talked about my nagging wife, the more my friends encouraged me to set her in her place. So I bashed her up! You can't blame me for it; I can't even remember it!"

They struck me, but I was not hurt! They beat me [as with a hammer], but I did not feel it! When shall I awake? I will crave and seek more wine again [and escape reality].
—PROVERBS 23:35, AMP

Although research shows that alcohol use is more prevalent among men than women, women are more vulnerable than men to alcohol-related organ damage and to legal and interpersonal difficulties. And binge drinking is most common among young women ages eighteen to twenty-five.[2]

I don't know about you, but I can see Satan abuse intricately at work in a person who is controlled by a spirit of addiction.

Increasing evidence points to a significant correlation between alcohol abuse and domestic violence, including sexual abuse. Alcohol is a central nervous system depressant, creating many different symptoms, such as a lack of social inhibition, poor impulse control, feelings of euphoria, poor coordination, and impaired judgment. Even though studies find that alcohol or drug abuse is not always a factor in violent/abusive behavior, and some alcoholics function very well when under the influence, it is frequently the influence that triggers violence.

Anger and hostility, as well as immature attempts at sexual/emotional fulfillment, are usually generated by negative communication between couples and other family members, and not directly by the intake of alcohol.

As Christians, no substance should control our lives. This subject is extremely important for discussion because of the widespread devastation that substance abuse, alcoholism, pornography, and child abuse are having in so many Christian marriages. Many wives are suffering silently. Many children are becoming victims of mental and physical abuse by an alcoholic or unfaithful father. Studies also indicate that more and more women are also abusing alcohol and different types of antidepressants and mood-enhancing medications.

The problem is massive and affecting an alarming rising number of families.

Alcoholism and drug abuse have become so prevalent that some authors have even tried to change the name to give hope to countless alcoholics. Their theory is that by simply espousing the belief that by changing the name and reframing the illness, the alcoholic victim will be able to get well. I have chosen to highlight this subject because it is such a predominant problem and heartache in so many homes.

ALCOHOL ADDICTION STATISTICS

- Americans suffering from alcoholism number 17.6 million.[3]

- Excessive alcohol consumption causes more than one million deaths each year.[4]

- Half of all auto fatalities are due to alcohol consumption.[5]

- Every day, more than ten thousand teenage kids try alcohol for the first time.[6]

- An estimated 6.6 million children live in households where one parent is an alcoholic.[7]

- The percentage of hospital admissions due to alcohol among women and adolescents is 20.8 percent.[8]

- There were 188,981 alcohol-related hospital admissions by patients ages twelve to twenty in 2008.[9]

- About 95 percent of alcoholics die from alcoholism disease, and on average they lose twenty-six years from their normal life expectancy.[10]

- About 30 percent of suicides is related to alcohol use.[11]

- Ninety-seven thousand college students were victims of alcohol-related sexual assault in 2009.[12]

- In one in three sexual assaults, the perpetrator was intoxicated.[13]

- In 2005, the total cost of alcohol dependence to the US economy was $220 billion.[14]

All addictions have something in common—they enslave and claim ownership of their victims. Everyone experiencing the ravages of this *monster demanding a human sacrifice* will find solace and healing in God's presence. There is no other force or source higher than the name of Jesus that can destroy the *monsters* that invade a person and destroy homes. You can't simply change the name or disguise an entity and expect healing to be manifested. The monsters of addiction have to be dealt with through spiritual warfare in the name of Jesus, and the victim has to be willing to participate in the warfare.

Substance abuse addiction is so enslaving that any Christian should be able to recognize the tremendous implication of an evil spirit at work in the addicted person's life. Society may believe that by changing the name of alcoholism or substance abuse to a different, better-sounding name, the person will feel better and even get well. But that is not the case. There is a spiritual force involved in the addiction. This demonic force has to be ousted, and the person has to be set free from the enslaving bondage. Spiritual deliverance by a seasoned and knowledgeable minister will be necessary to set the person free. Many programs are very effective and help people cope with the addictions, but they do not set them free. And for the person to remain free, he or she must make an about-face and leave behind all the things that led to the addiction. A free person has to walk, talk, and act like a new person. This also is spiritual warfare—refusing to go back to the pigpen.

> The use of alcohol will lower good judgment and reduce the individual's ability to know his own strength or show necessary restraint if an argument ensues. This lowered judgment leads to "accidents" between couples in the home. It will also decrease inhibitions. The person under the influence of alcohol or drugs can become bold in their assertions. The substance "gives permission" for the intoxicated person to say whatever comes to mind and do whatever tickles their fancy. This lack of social restraint can lead to all sorts of acting out behavior, including violence. Essentially, the drugs or alcohol give "permission" to impulsive feelings of rage and hostility, as well as to sexual/emotional acting out.[15]

FINDING FREEDOM FROM ENSLAVING ADDICTIONS

You may be wondering if a person can be set free from an enslaving addiction. I have a friend who was going through a very difficult situation with her husband and was placed in a position to have to make a drastic decision. Her husband had developed an addiction that was affecting the core and well-being of their marriage. The moment he came home, he would recede into his own little personal world, leaving her helplessly wondering if he would ever come back to reality. Even though he carried out all his duties at work and even attended church, intimacy with his wife was dead. The following is her testimony of the battle between good and evil and how she was able to overcome. She has encouraged me to share this, written in her own words, with my readers.

> There was a time when a situation in my marriage had progressed to the point that a line had to be drawn. After much seeking, counseling, and prayer over a significant period of time, the situation finally came to the point where my husband had to make a decision about whether he wanted to continue with a particular behavior or live with me. I spoke to

him and gave him a week to think, pray, and decide. I went to another state and joined an anger management class conducted by one of the foremost psychiatric hospitals dealing with addictions. I truly was not mad AT HIM, but I was very angry that I had been placed in the position of having to draw the line and stand the ground for recovery. I was risking a lot by leaving him to make the decision. My story is about an event that took place during the week-long counseling sessions that I was a part of. The facility I went to was not a Christ-centered facility, but top quality in the secular world. At the end of five days, every one in my small group was expected to go through a guided imagery session under the direction of a trained counselor.

The Gestalt method was implemented to allow the participants to release their anger at the individual who was the focal point of the situation that was causing the hurt and stored-up anger. Before the session I told the counselor that I was not trying to oppose the program or be out of order, but because I was a Christian, I did not believe that I could participate in guided imagery. She was very accommodating and said that I could participate in the activity without doing the guided imagery and that I should just join the group and see what happens. She would save me until last.

The process was to place a box of tissues in the participant's lap. Each sheet represented something they were to "let go." There was an empty chair placed in front of each participant, who was given a rubber or foam bat. The participants were given instructions to allow themselves to be drawn by the guided imagery until they began visualizing their "abusing person" siting in the chair. They were then allowed to do whatever was necessary to release their anger upon the visualized perpetrator while tearing off tissue after tissue as they expressed their anger and released the events. I think you get the picture here. That poor old chair took a real beating that day, and tissues were deep on the floor when it came my turn.

I had no idea if I would be able to participate at that time, but I took the bat and the tissues and began to stare at the chair. All of a sudden the actual enemy of my marriage materialized in that chair. I don't think it was all in my mind or imagination either. I took that bat and initiated an extremely violent attack against Satan. I told him in no uncertain terms that he would not take my marriage and that he was to depart from my household and never bring any accusation against my husband. I whacked that chair to pieces and told Satan that he had blinded the others in the room to believe that their anger should be directed at some person while all the time he was really the one behind all of the events. I told him that he was going to have to take a couple of good whacks from me on their behalf. I absolutely destroyed the bat and nearly broke the chair. I did not throw any tissues. I told Satan that I had nothing to let go of because I intended to release to God all of the memories of all he had done to wreak havoc in the lives of all those in that group. I expressed that I was angry with him and that I would hold on to all of my tissues and he better not come creeping around thinking that there was an ounce of forgiveness in me toward him.

I was never angry, nor did I take offense with my husband! My anger and offense were directed at the enemy, and I let him know that too. When I was done, every one in the room was wide-eyed and very still. I didn't plan it. I didn't think it out. But if you can get the vision of me whacking that chair and beating up on Satan himself, I hope that you can write it into your book with a lot more enthusiasm.

Not only has Satan never come back to haunt my husband on the tormenting issues, he can't even find another demon who wants to take on the assignment. One of the big differences in the effect for me as opposed to the others in the group was that they imagined the person as the focus of their anger. In my case Satan himself ACTUALLY got whacked, and today, several years later, my husband and I are enjoying the victory.

Spiritual warfare against addictions

This testimony brings to my mind the true meaning of the scripture in Ephesians 6:12 (AMP):

> For we are not wrestling with flesh and blood [contending only with physical opponents], but against the despotisms, against the powers, against [the master spirits who are] the world rulers of this present darkness, against the spirit forces of wickedness in the heavenly (supernatural) sphere.

Our marriages will not be able to survive the attacks of the enemy and the myriads of temptations invading our atmosphere unless we literally engage in *spiritual warfare* and practice walking in love and unity as a consistent and committed lifestyle.

If I were to choose the most important thing as the key that has kept my marriage united and healthy, I would have to say it is loving my husband and family more than myself and practicing *spiritual warfare* EVERY DAY!

I can hear some of you younger ones asking, "What is spiritual warfare, and how do you practice it every day?"

The word *spiritual* means, "unworldly, divine-heavenly, nonphysical, transcendent, etc." The word *warfare* means, "conflict, fighting, combat, rivalry, and war." To effectively engage in spiritual warfare, you must first walk in purity. By that I mean that a person must have a clean conscience and do everything possible to please God and obey His Word. Obeying God is trusting Him with your life. Don't turn me off yet. This process is easier to achieve than living a life of defeat.

Since we are spiritual beings, we cannot direct our combat against a human person. It has to be against the evil spirits that come to disrupt, abuse, and drive people into slavery. Jesus has already delegated to all believers power and authority over *all* demonic influence.

> Behold! I have given you authority and power to trample upon serpents and scorpions, and [physical and mental strength and ability] over all the power that the enemy [possesses]; and nothing shall in any way harm you.
>
> —LUKE 10:19, AMP

Just like my friend who whacked the enemy with a bat and her powerful words, refusing to direct her warfare against her husband, we too can open our mouth fearlessly and wage war by applying pertinent scriptures and learning to pray powerful prayers against the evil spirits that come to destroy our loved ones. Perhaps you don't have a serious problem right now, but don't wait until you do. Prepare ahead.

John Eckhardt has several books on warfare prayers that will be invaluable teachings on this subject.[16]

I can't end this subject without warning you that if you complain, nag, and hold a grudge, even if you do spiritual warfare day and night, *nothing is going to happen*. Your heart must be surrendered. You must allow God's love to rule you. There has to be a *knowing* in your heart that after you have done everything possible, if your loved one decides to walk away from God and the relationship, you will be rewarded for your faithfulness. The storm will have an ending, and God will sustain you.

Control of the imagination

One of Satan's strongholds lies in the *imagination*. Some of you have suffered from your "vivid imagination" from childhood, and it is a marvelous gospel that brings you light as to how you may be set free from an inflamed imagination. Perhaps you have daydreams—your mind carries you away against your will; or mental pictures—awful pictures of things that are going to happen—until you can scarcely endure it; or you once saw something dreadful happen, and for the rest of your life you are haunted by it. You have asked God to take it away. You have shut your mind, closed your eyes, refused to look—but with no relief. Then the enemy has told you lies about it—said you were "born with a vivid imagination" or that it is "natural." But it can all be stopped and lifelong suffering ended by recognizing that it is an evil spirit flashing these pictures into the imagination.[17]

Praying is *work*. Pray *out* the obstacles, pray *in* the positive power.[18]

Freedom comes when you have knowledge and reject what is not of God. The moment an evil spirit is recognized and commanded to go in the name of Jesus, he must leave. The power of the Holy Spirit in the person is the force that drives evil out. Go deeper on this subject. Start practicing warfare praying, and commit yourself to educating your mind and spirit by memorizing scriptures and asking the Holy Spirit to train you.

RESISTING THE DEVIL IN THE WILDERNESS

We must learn to talk back to the devil the same as Jesus did in the wilderness by quoting the Word, "It is written!", and renouncing his tricks. The battle today is for the family and the home. Most families live in continuous strife, division, confusion, and contention caused by Satan and his tactics against them.

Warfare is not only prayer. There is no purpose in petitioning God for something He has already given us. No wonder so many prayers go unanswered. We must stop storming heaven for what is already provided—*authority over all the power of the enemy.* All evil and unclean spirits must be purged from our lives. For restoration to take place, there must be a cleansing process, a clearing away of the old garbage in our lives.

The cause of a problem is usually due to both the presence of a demon and the weakness of the flesh (Gal. 5:19–21). We must be fruit-bearing Christians in order to be in the will of God and partake of His blessings.

Love is a special target for the enemy since it is the first and principal fruit of the Spirit as well as a commandment. Demons of resentment can defeat love in a person's life if that person refuses to forgive offenses. Rejection is the most common demon spirit, because people affected by this spirit have not been properly loved, and as a result, they find it hard to love others.

The warfare against marriage is very real. Christians need to become aware and knowledgeable of their rights as believers to be able to withstand and resist the enemy. As time goes by, the war against evil will increase, and everyone we know will be affected in one way or the other. We must not be afraid but prepared and equipped. It begins with training. Fear has to be cast out, and love must rule in our homes.

CHAPTER NINE

PROTECT YOUR HOME WITH A SECURITY SYSTEM

Girding up your marriage

Now gird up your loins like a man...

—JOB 38:3, NAS

JUST AS A thief enters an unguarded home and steals, kills, and devours, so it is in a home where the Spirit of God and the protection of God's angels are not dwelling. I am convinced that without a spiritual security system built upon the Word of God, our homes cannot and will not be able to withstand the even tougher, perilous times of crisis ahead of us

All the advanced technology and outlets of information available to us have produced incredible amounts of information and resources pertaining to marriage and parenting. A lot of it is beneficial, but most of it follows the ways of the world and is not based upon the Word of God.

God intended for our homes to be a flourishing garden, full of life and substance, material wealth, and personal enjoyment. But Eve allowed herself to be tempted by the devil, and since that time we are in warfare with good and evil.

We must reclaim our homes and establish a firm foundation upon

Jesus Christ, the solid rock. Stop giving the enemy permission to express himself in your marriage. Take a stand. "Resist the devil and he will flee from you" (James 4:7).

To become a powerful Christian, one must first receive training and discipleship. Without this process of preparation, a Christian remains vulnerable to the attacks of the enemy and ignorant of his rights in Christ Jesus.

The same process applies to a husband and wife. Without prior preparation and instruction of what a Christian marriage is all about, they will be poised for disillusionment and many setbacks. I can compare the end result to be like one of the couples competing in *Dancing With the Stars*. If they wait until they get to the actual competition without practicing and preparing ahead, they will surely be in for a huge flop. But if they practice and learn all the different moves and techniques, and if they exercise every muscle until they are sure that they are sure, then they can compete for the prize.

Knowing your partner and knowing how he or she feels about life, God, work, money, children, and the future take time, intuitiveness, communication, and discernment. This kind of knowledge does not come automatically. It is not inherent but learned. I have wondered many times why this subject of marriage and parenting is not taught as a mandatory class in all high schools. But again, if this crucial teaching is not based upon the Word of God, it will lack the most important asset: the necessity of the power of Christ in us to withstand every attack of the enemy.

Marital love and harmony are not something we conjure up or try to make happen. God, our heavenly Father, created us with the capacity to love and delight each other.

A WOMAN'S DELIGHTS

In the Song of Solomon 7:6, the man says: "How fair and how pleasant you are, O love, *with your delights!*" (emphasis added). God created every woman with a delightful foundation of love within her. This love and devotion the Creator placed within us has to be developed and cultivated like seed to be enjoyed.

The fruit of the Spirit (Gal. 5:22–23, AMP) that is produced in us releases the delights of:

- *Love* (to adore, strong affection, desire, passionate attraction, beloved, worship of God, God's love for humanity)

- *Joy* (gladness, delight, happiness, pleasure, enjoyment)

- *Peace* (calm, harmony, concord, reconciliation, freedom from strife)

- *Patience* (an even temper, forbearance, endurance, tolerance, fortitude, staying power, lack of complaint, stamina)

- *Kindness* (compassion, consideration, gentleness, kindheartedness, sympathy, thoughtfulness, helpfulness, charity)

- *Goodness* (benevolence, virtuousness, gosh, gee, wow, oh my)

- *Faithfulness* (loyalty, authenticity, realism, closeness, accuracy, fidelity, unwavering in belief, consistently loyal, not adulterous or promiscuous, conscientious)

- *Gentleness* (meekness, humility, quietness, tenderness)

- *Self-control* (self-restraint, continence, discipline, willpower, moderation)

All these attributes are the fruit of the Holy Spirit (the work that His presence within accomplishes).

Now really take a good look at the fruit described in this passage. Can you mark off the fruit operating in your life right now? Be honest with yourself, and see what is lacking. Take it a step further and determine in your heart that you want to see ALL the fruit of the Holy Spirit actively working in you. It will transform the way you see life and the way you think, act, feel, and speak.

We all know that too many families everywhere are in a state of crisis, walking on a dangerously fast treadmill of survival.

THE CHURCH AND YOUR HOME ARE SHELTERS

God has established the church and the home as the two primary sources of protection and shelter from the perils of sin and the torment of the enemy. The choice is placed before us. It is not vague or hidden. Choosing to live life in the covering of God's shadow, or choosing to live life in the open, unprotected field where Satan has free range, is all up to us.

Young couples need to learn the importance of doing everything in their power to manage their homes with wisdom and understanding. Lack of knowledge will cause strife and misunderstanding in any relationship. The only way a young couple is going to learn how to function with wisdom and understanding is by getting grounded in a dynamic Bible-believing church. Not only will you learn how to apply godly principles in your marriage, but you will also become part of a larger Christian family that will reach out to you when the need arises. A young couple should stay actively connected with other Christian couples. They should also join a Bible class to receive spiritual nourishment. Following this advice will protect you from experiencing serious setbacks.

Serving God and loving each other as a committed couple will have an everlasting dynamic effect on everything and everyone you contact. God is specific, organized, intentional, and holy. His promises are for His children. His blessings are infinite and abundant.

God is anxiously waiting on us to stay fixed on His solid foundation so that He can extravagantly bless us. Now that is worth every effort to receive training and get prepared to live like children of royalty!

I like what Acts 16:31 (AMP) says, and I consider this truth as my safety net:

> Believe in the Lord Jesus Christ [give yourself up to Him, take yourself out of your own keeping and entrust yourself into His keeping] and you will be saved, [and this applies both to] you and your household as well.

A radical change is necessary to transplant the old way of thinking and doing things. We get so used to doing things the same way all the time that we become like addicts who have a hard time making changes to do things differently. We need a heart revolution that will totally launch us out of our selfish mind-set into the freedom of the fullness of Christ and a total commitment to each other.

Selfishness and hesitancy of embracing change keeps so many married couples in a dull rut. It's the same monotonous thing, day in and day out. There is so much to enjoy in a marriage that has God's stamp of approval on it. *Don't underestimate living under God Almighty's rule. It's supreme living at it's best.*

During all my years of counseling, I have observed many marriages fall apart, some ending in long separations or divorce. I have also observed many marriages sold out to Christ who have experienced great loss and many difficult challenges in their lives, but the marriage partners have remained committed to each other.

Please take this advice seriously. *If you want a fulfilling, lasting marriage, you must always make Jesus Christ the primary source.* He must become your security and your assurance. Your spouse will look up to you. Your children will be a reward and not a headache. You will leave an inheritance that will affect generations to come.

Set apart some time to identify the flow *of hindrances and torments.*

The woman with the "flow" of blood had to actively seek out and look for Jesus to receive her healing (Luke 8:43–44). We must also seek out Jesus and actively implement a strategic plan to oust the enemy who has been intensely involved in destroying so many marriages.

Spiritual warfare is active, not passive. Even if you have a wonderful marriage, spiritual warfare must be part of your daily regimen to ward off the strategies of the enemy.

To gird up means to get yourself ready, to prepare yourself to do something difficult and challenging. What I am trying to convey through this phrase is the urgent task a Christian married couple has to be spiritually ready at all times and to surround and cover their relationship with prayer and the power of the blood of Jesus. This is serious business. It can't be left for when the ship is sinking and the storms are devouring your marriage.

Build your house upon the instructions and counsel in the Word of God, and you'll have a solid foundation. When the storms come and the big bad wolf tries to blow your marriage away, no devil in hell will be able to tear your house down. Your security system will be in place (Matt. 7:24–25).

THE PRACTICE OF SPIRITUAL WARFARE

When you think of spiritual warfare, you may think of demons, exorcism, rebuking, intercession, deliverance, warfare praying, and such. I believe that obeying the Ten Commandments, being kind and generous, manifesting the fruit of the Spirit, walking away from temptation, and saying NO to sin are actions of spiritual warfare. Putting on the whole armor of God, which is Jesus Christ in us, is also spiritual warfare.

The practice of spiritual warfare has to be a lifestyle. Getting good at praying, making vows, confessing and declaring specific scriptures, binding and loosing, and reading the Bible every day while turning on the anger, fear, and doubt switches at the same time is not effective spiritual warfare.

Spiritual warfare is:

- Loving your spouse

- Keeping order in your life and home

- Refusing to complain and become bitter

- Being a good steward of your money

- Loving difficult people

- Forgiving those who hurt you

- Disciplining your children

- Serving and loving God with all your heart

- Applying spiritual principles and obeying them

As you can see, all of the above, and more, involve action. When we take action, God takes action! This God-lifestyle keeps us in enmity with the spirit of Satan and opens the doors of blessing. God has promised to perform His Word in us when we obey and believe it. Wrapped up in this God-lifestyle, we can confidently declare, "Satan, you can't have my marriage, my children, my inheritance, my finances, my health, or my substance."

Lester Sumrall says it this way: "Pray militantly. Develop a militant voice. Give militantly. Resist the enemy militantly; and love militantly."[1]

DON'T NEGLECT YOUR SPIRITUAL ALTAR

Go to your spiritual altar every day. Choose a place. Let it be your bedside, a chair, your walk-in closet, the bathroom, the garage, your car...be creative. But make it the same place every day. Surrender there to God daily.

> We have an altar [or a sacred tent].
>
> —HEBREWS 13:10

Wash yourself clean.

In God's presence we wash ourselves clean. Your devotional time is just as important as brushing your teeth, and it should become a daily habit. To render praise and worship to our magnificent God and Father is a privilege and an honor—and it is also an honor to thank Him and confess and acknowledge Him. God is ready to perform His Word when we come to Him with praise and adoration, declaring His Word (have a list of scriptures that minister deeply to you, such as for healing; believing for a husband, son, daughter, a job, or business; and so forth). Read this section a few times. Don't get bored. This advice is life because the Word of God is life to all who find it and medicine to all their bodies (Prov. 4:22).

The Word you speak in faith is living water, and it will wash you and sanctify you as you speak it in faith. Praying, praising, and worshiping God the Father, Jesus the Son, and the Holy Spirit are acts of sacrifice because our flesh constantly desires to be gratified, pampered, and indulged.

Don't go by your feelings. This practice of praying and declaring God's Word is as important as remembering to take your vitamins and minerals. It is as important as going to work and paying your rent, and more important than your exercise routine or eating your meals. By practicing this spiritual discipline, you will become stronger and more energetic and will acquire wisdom and knowledge to make wise decisions and choices.

Your discernment, which means your "understanding," will be exercised, developed, and tested. Your speech will improve. Your relationships will become healthier. Your intuition will help you make wise decisions. Wisdom will rise up to meet you. Wow! Talk about developing your spiritual muscles!

> True wisdom and real power belong to God; from him we learn how to live, and also what to live for.
>
> —JOB 12:13, THE MESSAGE

Let me ask you a question: When was the last time you felt good and content *all day long*? This practice of a relationship with your Maker will definitely enhance your well-being. It will give you peace of mind, sharpen your God-given skills and abilities, and greatly improve and maintain your family relationships.

We were created for fellowship with Father God. Christ Jesus is always interceding for us (Rom. 8:34). The Holy Spirit receives our supplications (our prayers) and intercedes for us *with groanings too deep for words* (Rom 8:26, NAS). Now that is outstanding news. Both Jesus and the Holy Spirit are praying, supplicating, pleading, yearning, and groaning for your well-being and your salvation. That is an awesome thought and mental picture. How selfish can we be, or how insensitive, to neglect this spiritual relationship? What are we doing for ourselves?

Many of us are having our frequent pity parties: *Oh me, oh my, I don't know how I am going to make it today! I can't believe this is happening to me!* Hey, friend, it's time to end this barrage of helplessness and get up—put on your warrior boots and be the "more than an overcomer" the Word talks about and you sometimes quote, the one you were created to become. The power of God is already residing in you!

Don't be asking for a lot of stuff. He knows what your needs are, and He has already made provision. "The Lord is my Shepherd...I shall not lack" (Ps. 23:1, AMP). He's already made provision for you.

Now I want you to pay close attention to all these things I am telling you. Don't just read these words and forget them. This advice is not supposed to just tickle your ears and make you feel interested for a little while or make you feel guilty because you're not consistent in this area. No! You must determine in your mind and heart that you want to develop and exercise your spiritual inner man so that it becomes stronger than your natural self, than your soul man.

All your decisions should be based on what God says in His Word. There should be a lining of wisdom in all you do and say. Other people such as your friends, family, children, and coworkers should look up to you and desire to be around you. They should want to ask you for prayer when they have a need because God's wisdom and understanding are ruling your life and are evident for all to see.

Oh, you may think that is impossible to achieve. You may battle with negative thoughts. Well, take confidence. I did too! It will take one step at a time, one prayer at a time, one verse and scripture at a time, and one moment of privacy in your personal altar in God's presence at a time. God doesn't take naps. He's always waiting for you. The Holy Spirit is the enabler, your helper, your friend, and your teacher (John 14:26). You have nothing to lose and much to gain. God already put ability in you to become strong, positive, healthy, wealthy, and able to do all things above and beyond what your little finite mind can comprehend.

Allow the Holy Spirit to stretch you and teach you how to become strong, vivacious, healthy, fearless of the attacks of the enemy, and capable of achieving those things you have thought in your mind are impossible to achieve but desire. The Spirit of God supplies us with intelligence, wisdom, and inspiration (Acts 6:10). When you are in Christ, and His Spirit dwells in you, you are full of grace, divine blessing, favor, power, strength, and ability. And the miraculous is also at work in you (Acts 6:8). Being led by the Spirit of God grants you the privilege of becoming His possession, His son or daughter of royalty (Rom. 8:14).

Chapter Ten

THE HEALING POWER OF FRIENDSHIP AND INTIMACY

Channel healthy emotions into your marriage

My lover is mine, and I am his.
—Song of Solomon 2:16, The Message

Love and intimacy between married couples signify ownership. Just as our love for God qualifies us for intimacy and ownership by Him, so does a married couple become one when they vow their love to each other (1 Cor. 8:3, AMP).

My husband's favorite little lyric about intimacy is "into-me-you-see." Knowing what is inside of our mate's heart is so important. This comes about when we develop a close and intimate relationship with each other.

Intimacy can be described as:

- Familiarity

- Closeness

- Understanding

- Confidence

- Caring

- Tenderness

- Affection

- A close relationship

- Quiet atmosphere

- Private utterance or action

- Sexual act

My intention is not to write all about sex and how it's done, but I would like to concentrate on the need all married couples have for genuine friendship and enjoyable intimacy. Many books have been written on this subject of sex, and it will be beneficial for us to read many of them and learn to apply the things that will improve our sex lives.

I was raised in a very strict and legalistic home and got married in 1970. I was molested as a child and ignorant of everything that had to do with romance, intimacy, and marital sex. Reading was my favorite hobby, and I decided to pour myself into all the books on marriage that I could borrow from the library. I remember buying a Christian book that changed my attitude about marriage forever after I was touched by reading the words on the back cover:

- Marriage is a gift.

- Marriage is an opportunity for love to be learned.

- Marriage is a call to servanthood.

- Marriage is a call to friendship.

- Marriage is a call to suffering.

- Marriage is a refining process. It is an opportunity to be refined by God into the person He wants us to be.

- Marriage is not an event but a way of life.

The author also wrote: "Whereas romantic love cannot sustain a relationship, *companionship or friendship-love can*....It's when the fulfillment of his or her needs becomes one of your needs. Friendship-love involves a certain level of intimacy in which there is openness, vulnerability, and emotional connection....A marriage that lasts is a marriage that has a husband and wife who are friends."[1]

Thousands of people today are getting a perverted image of what marriage is from the world's portrayal of marriage. As one example, according to a survey by the Romance Writers of America in 2009, 74.8 million Americans read at least one romance novel in the past year, with romance readers more likely to be married or involved in a relationship.[2]

I've spoken with young married women whose lives have been deeply affected by their emotional involvement in romance novels. They find themselves playing the part of the heroine in the novels during the times of sexual intimacy with their own mates. This is very dangerous and leads to unfulfilled needs. This kind of fantasy involvement is not what God intended as healthy intimacy between a husband and wife. I recall a young wife confessing to me that even when she ate a banana or an apple, she felt as if she was having sexual intimacy with the fruit she was eating. Many people are living double personalities due to the influence of romance novels. This topic is affecting many Christians as well, and they wonder why they are having problems in their marriage.

"ALL HE WANTS IS SEX"

Perhaps you've heard a married woman say, "All he wants is sex." Most of the time this is true. God created man to enjoy his wife and to release his tensions and passions through sexual intercourse with her. And God created woman with the ability to participate and enjoy the act. When a man enters a woman, they both become one flesh. Don't miss out on the power of your influence to improve your sex life. It just may be the best power tool you can use to transform your marriage into a healthy and happy one.

If sex has become a difficult area to talk about in your marriage, it is possible that your husband is hungry for an intimate and satisfying union with you. The problem with too many men is that touch is touch, and it all feels the same and leads to arousal, but it's not the case for his wife. Rubbing her back and massaging her feet may cause arousal, and he may think he's entering the delight zone, but she thinks he's helping her relax and relieve the pain in her muscles. Women need to educate their man in this area, or it will become a constant discouragement for their man and for her. Physical touch that doesn't end in sex is intimate loving affection, and women need and love this kind of touch, especially when they have had a controversial or hectic day. Every woman is complex and different. Men need to learn to *know* their wives and what makes them enjoy their time together by paying attention and experimenting. If it works, try it again.

> Body contact shows possession. When we have close intimate body contact with another human being, there is a form of transference of self and possession that occurs. That is why we need to be so careful with whom we share our bodies.[3]

To really enjoy intimacy, a woman must learn to understand her man. Men don't want to become women. Women love to talk, open up, enjoy details, and remember lots of things, and they would love to share everything that goes on when their husband comes home, just as they enjoy doing with their girlfriends. Most men don't want to hear all that. God made them different, praise God!

WHY ARE WOMEN SO UNHAPPY?

Much is written about women being the ones unhappy with their marriages. There is so little understanding of the roles God created for men and women that it is no wonder that intimacy is out the door in so many of today's marriages.

Some women complain about their husband's lack of interest in sexual intimacy. There may be several reasons, such as erectile dysfunction, a recovering porn addict, a secret homosexual relationship, or a habit of masturbation. Any of these reasons, among others, could very well quench the desire for sexual intimacy in a man for his wife, and in a woman for her husband as well. Talking about it will open the door to receive professional help. Unless these issues are discussed in the open, the problem will only get worse.

Mark Gungor, a pastor, author, and motivational speaker, says: "In most cases, it is women who are upset with the whole marriage enterprise. Eighty percent of all divorces are filed by women. It is usually the woman who seeks out marriage counseling. Women of our day are the ones frustrated to the hilt. It is the woman who always seems to have her heart broken. It is the woman who is the most disappointed. I now believe women of the twenty-first century have completely unrealistic expectations when it comes to dealing with and living with men. And I am convinced divorce rates will continue to rise if women do not bring their expectations about marriage back to reality. Unrealistic expectations are often the culprits responsible for misery women feel—not their husbands. The unsustainable, unreasonable romantic longings of women are ripping marriages apart."[4]

APPLY POSITIVE WORDS AND A TENDER TOUCH

Intimacy in marriage cannot be attained if there are lots of negative words, grunts, yelling, slamming doors, walking out in the middle of a conversations, no eye contact, and one marriage partner who is being just plain obnoxious. Sexual intimacy begins with a tender touch, an affectionate embrace, and alluring positive words, and it ends in a blissful orgasm and a satisfying affection for each other.

Most affairs start because of lack of affection for the woman and lack of sex for the man. As a couple continues to play the game of *he doesn't love me, she doesn't give me enough*, they will both lose until the game is over. When your marriage is struggling in the area of intimacy, check your affection and attention levels.

The more good words spoken between a couple, the better their intimacy will get. Lots of bad words will only push each mate further apart. When you first started out, you did everything together—dinner, bowling, ball games, driving, the movies, church, and just about everything. A few years go by, and it's not the same anymore. Busyness takes over, and the relationship begins to suffer. Beware of your priorities. Never underestimate your social and emotional needs.

Most people tend to lash out or lecture during stressful times, especially if the predicament is somebody else's fault.

Gary Smalley and John Trent express it this way: "But tenderness, above and beyond the call of our human nature, is a transformer, an energizer of those around us....I wasn't aware that softness during stressful times was even an option until several years into my marriage. And that's when I learned that one of a person's greatest needs is to be comforted, especially during moments in life when the roof falls in."[5]

A man who is privileged to have a loving and respectful wife who is able to create an atmosphere free from bitterness and strife will be able to meet the storms of life with optimism, even when the future seems uncertain.

Positive words and tender touches are precursors to wonderful romantic intimacy.

Come on now! Whether you have a good marriage, a so-so marriage, a boring one, or a dead one, start applying some of these principles. Become demonstrative, intimate, active, outward bound, and fervent in your admiration, your words, and your actions. Apply all the little things that help edify and produce a healthy and fulfilled marriage and home to your own relationship. Your children will inherit and reap the benefits as they continue imitating and living out the same example. A good and happy home will become the inheritance you leave your children and those you influence.

Forget about your rights and the things you have always dreamed or expected in a marriage relationship. Start sowing positive and faith-filled seeds into your marital relationship. This is what spiritual warfare is all about. This is what God truly intended for us. It means going against your own will and flesh, against peer pressures, and against all the ungodly examples we see every day in the media and all around us. We are either blessed by God's goodness or cursed by Satan's devices and strategies for our marriage and family. Again, we choose!

Start declaring right now: Satan, you can't have my marriage!

YOU CAN HAVE A
SUPERNATURAL MARRIAGE

STAYING CONNECTED TO the source of life and living in Christ involves more than going to church, listening to Christian TV, saying a few prayers, and reading a few scriptures. It's more than listening to Christian music and teaching CDs and getting excited over a prophetic word or good preaching. It is more than taking lots of notes and using the keys of binding and loosing. It is more than going to a Bible school or teaching a seminary class. It is more than a theological title or degree. All these things are good, but it is what we do after we do all these things that really impresses God to bless us with all His riches in glory.

To have a blessed supernatural marriage, you must know and do the things in the rulebook of God's Word. It's that simple, yet so many couples think that their lives will be too boring or too demanding. Living under the supernatural covering of God's blessing guarantees the strength and wisdom to overcome temptations and difficulties. The thesaurus describes *supernatural* as something mystic and magical. The dictionary gives this definition: "paranormal, not of natural world, relating to deity." Walking in the supernatural power of the kingdom of heaven makes all of God's resources and treasures available to your marriage.

What does this all have to do with marriage? Everything. A

marriage that is not plugged into and connected to God is one that sooner or later will experience a meltdown and the attacks of the enemy.

What attacks? Indifference, lukewarmness, control, manipulation, ego problems, small white lies, insatiable desires, mistrust, suspicion, and all the things the enemy uses to bring destruction, some of which were described in these pages. All these evil qualities are rooted in disobedience and self-will.

THE TREASURE IS IN YOU!

Treasure means, "gems, money, to cherish, value, to appreciate, take pleasure in, and to regard as valuable." It also means a pearl of great value and a prize.

A treasure is something of great value. To value something, you must pay attention to it. Lack of attention is neglect. Negligence is lack of care and application. Healthy and happy marriages thrive and succeed when they are consistently fed love and attention.

Change and growth are impossible if you always do things the same way you have always done them and neglect to pay attention to the red warning flags. Many of us choose to hold and hide painful and afflicting torments and memories of issues we are suffering or suffered in the past. We hold on to abuse, offenses, and mistreatments as if they are precious and valuable treasures.

As we hold on to our burdens, we forget about our successes, our good health, the joy of children, the good deeds others have done for us, and God's promise to bless and keep us. We have a hard time forgetting the wounds and hurts of the past.

> In the house of the [uncompromisingly] righteous is great [priceless] treasure.
>
> —PROVERBS 15:6, AMP

The "house" this scripture talks about is not your physical house but your spiritual house. A Christian is the temple of the Holy Spirit, and God's priceless treasure dwells in you! Christ in you, your hope of glory. Jesus is the Word. Salvation, peace, the gifts of the Holy Spirit, authority in the name of Jesus, all this priceless treasure dwells in you. Not only are you God's peculiar possession and treasure, but also His treasure, Christ Jesus, dwells in you.

> If you will obey My voice in truth and keep My covenant, *then you shall be My own peculiar possession and treasure* from among and above all peoples; for all the earth is Mine.
> —EXODUS 19:5, AMP, EMPHASIS ADDED

Everything that belongs to God is available to you. God desires to bless you with His treasures of love, peace, confidence, health, strength, joy, wisdom, understanding, knowledge, provision, and abundance. He desires that you have a wonderful and successful marriage and family.

There is a requirement. You must first allow Him to clean out of you all the *garbage* such as impurity, hate, jealousy, offenses, bad habits, rooted resentments, fear, phobias, discord, gossip, bitterness, all forms of anger, and enmity. All these impure things attract demons and destroy marriages.

You can't get clean on your own. You need the help of the Holy Spirit. Don't underestimate the power of these words. They will be life to you if you heed them. Don't neglect God's awesome treasure in you. If you're facing problems, read this section a few times until you absorb and understand the importance of leaving the past behind and enjoying your heavenly treasures.

If your problems are present tense, and you're right now going through distresses, put into action the godly counsel in this book and find a godly couple to help you pray and give you counsel. Doing nothing will not enable you to get out of the enemy's trap. Like a mouse in a trap, your fate will remain in the enemy's territory.

We are spirit, soul, and body. What we feed our spirit will take root in our hearts and will determine how we think and what comes out of our mouth.

When you accept Jesus Christ as your Savior, you accept the treasure! God puts at your disposition the treasures of the kingdom of God to live a victorious life, no matter what has transpired in your past. I can hear Him telling you, "I want you to let go of your heavy burdens of junk that Satan has you carrying around all this time—that heavy baggage of suffering and emotional distress."

My mother suffered many injustices from an ungodly husband. She could have accepted the heavy burdens the enemy came to deposit upon her every day, but she chose to believe God and accept His treasures. It wasn't easy, but at the end, she has been the recipient of many gifts from God, and today, at age eighty-three, she continues to be a light in the darkness.

My destiny was at a crossroad. At the age of eighteen my heart felt divided. The choice was mine to either follow the example of my godly praying mother or rebel against God. The tormenting memories of an abusive father kept dancing before my eyes like little impious monsters trying to corner me into a mere existence.

I chose to enjoy the treasures of the kingdom of God. I refused to continue being a slave to my past abuse and injustices. I refused the curses that always come with abuse of any kind. Children inherit the sins of their parents. Repentance and renunciation are necessary to be set free.

You won't hear these words come out of my mouth: "I can't do this." "I am sick." "Oh, no, I'm afraid of that." "I fear that's impossible." "That's too much." "I'll never make it."

We all leave an inheritance whether we choose to or not. It

happens automatically. We have the treasure in us—Christ Jesus dwelling in the believer.

You may need healing and deliverance from abuse and oppression. Only in the presence of God can you find healing and wholeness. Begin by praying prayers that will make you clean and bring you back to your original state of innocence and righteousness.

> Then he will pray to God, and He will accept him, that he may see His face with joy, and He may restore His righteousness to man.
>
> —Job 33:26, NAS

God will restore your right, your reason, your virtues, what belongs to you, your joy, your childhood, and your treasures. Take one step at a time. Get ready to experience joy and peace.

THE WAY OF LOVE

Hannah Hurnard impressed me deeply with her account of her encounter with God's voice loving on her during a time of resentment, bitterness, and humiliation.

> All my life since then I have cherished like a jewel that little phrase which so suddenly shone into my dark, troubled mind, "A better way, the way of love." I cried out, however, at once, "But Lord, I can't walk that way. It isn't that I don't want to; it is simply that I can't. I want to love, and I want to act lovingly, but I fail the whole time because I don't feel loving. I feel only furious and hurt and humiliated and wanting to escape. And my nerves can't bear the strain. I feel at breaking point all the time. I want to follow the way of love, but I don't believe I could crawl along it on my hands and knees in this case. It is beyond me." And He said: "It is better to go stumbling and weeping and crawling like a worm along the way of love than to give it up and choose some other way."
>
> And so I started crawling, literally crawling, along the way of love, inwardly weeping a great deal, and stumbling most of

143

the time because I felt so sorry for myself, but learning for the first time that love, real love, is not primarily a feeling at all, but a thing of the will. A determination to act as I would if I felt all the delight of loving deeply and happily. For I found that if one acts in love, sooner or later one comes to feel all the joy and ecstasy of love.

NOTES

CHAPTER 1
MARRIAGE TODAY

1. Stephanie Samuel, "Americans Rank Top Immoral 'Sins' in New Poll," *The Christian Post*, June 1, 2011, http://www.christianpost.com/news/americans-rank-top-immoral-sins-in-new-poll-50715/ (accessed August 30, 2011).

2. *Quirk's* staff, "Is the 'Modern' Family the Model Family for Quality Time?", *Quirk's* e-newsletter, May 24, 2011, http://www.quirks.com/articles/2011/20110526-3.aspx (accessed August 30, 2011).

3. Doug Carlson, "Empire State Strikes Against Marriage," Ethics and Religious Liberty Commission, June 29, 2011, http://erlc.com/article/empire-state-strikes-against-marriage/ (accessed August 30, 2011).

4. Iris Delgado, *Satan, You Can't Have My Children* (Lake Mary, FL: Charisma House, 2011).

5. C. M. Ward, *Husbands and Wives* (n.p.: Revivaltime, 1976), 23.

CHAPTER 2
INVESTMENTS FOR FAITHFULNESS

1. Ken Chant, *Sitting on Top of the World* (n.p.: Ken Chant Ministries, 1991), 70.

2. Kathryn Kuhlman, *Nothing Is Impossible With God* (Alachua, FL: Bridge-Logos, 1992), 45.

3. Stan E. DeKoven, *Marriage and Family Life* (Ramona, CA: Vision Publishing, 2007), 174–175.

4. Richard D. Dobbins, *Invisible Imprint* (Camp Sherman, OR: VMI Publishers, 2002), 87.

5. Gary Smalley, *Love Is a Decision* (Nashville: Thomas Nelson, 2001), 78.

6. Ibid., 79.

7. John Marks Templeton, *Discovering the Laws of Life* (New York: Continuum Publishing, 1994), 297.

8. ThinkExist.com, "Booker T. Washington Quotes," http://thinkexist.com/quotation/i_shall_allow_no_man_to_belittle_my_soul_by/199954.html (accessed August 30, 2011).

9. Erwin W. Lutzer, *Making the Best of a Bad Decision* (Wheaton, IL: Tyndale, 2011), 62.

10. Chant, *Sitting on Top of the World*, 76.

11. Lutzer, *Making the Best of a Bad Decision*, 59.

CHAPTER 3
DIGGING OUT DESTRUCTIVE, HARMFUL ROOTS

1. Lou Priolo, *Divorce: Before You Say "I Don't"* (Phillipsburg, NJ: P&R, 2007), 5–6.

2. Kay Arthur, *A Marriage Without Regret* (Eugene, OR: Harvest House, 2000), 150.

CHAPTER 4
AFFAIR AND DIVORCE PREVENTION

1. Encarta Dictionary, MSN.com, s.v. "lasciviousness." No longer available online.

CHAPTER 5
KEEPING A FINANCIALLY STABLE HOME

1. Richard Carlson, *Don't Worry, Make Money* (New York: Hyperion, 1997), 9.

2. John Cummuta, *Debt Elimination 101* (Nashville, TN: Nelson Books, 2006), 33–34.

CHAPTER 6
LOVE AND BLESS *OUT LOUD*!

1. Paul R. Amato, "Interpreting Divorce Rates, Marriage Rates, and Data on the Percentage of Children with Single Parents,"

National Healthy Marriage Resource Center, January 1, 2010, http://www.healthymarriageinfo.org/resource-detail/index .aspx?rid=3284 (accessed August 31, 2011).

2. Grace Naismith, "What Doctors Can Do to Promote Fertility," Tyler Medical Clinic, http://www.tylermedicalclinic.com/ whatdoctorscandotopromotefertility.html (accessed September 1, 2011).

3. Center for Reproduction and Women's Health Care, "Male Infertility," http://www.houstonfertilityspecialist.com/male_ infertility.html (accessed September 1, 2011).

CHAPTER 7
HOW TO GROW A POWERFUL MARRIAGE

1. Ward, *Husbands and Wives*, 7.

2. Ibid., 6–7.

3. Delgado, *Satan, You Can't Have My Children*, 90.

4. Ibid., 84.

CHAPTER 8
IS SATAN ABUSE TROUBLING YOUR MARRIAGE?

1. T. M. Johnson, *Baker Encyclopedia of Psychology* (Grand Rapids, MI: Baker Book House, 1985), 1128.

2. Bill Urell, "Are Women More Vulnerable to Alcohol's Effects?", Addiction Recovery Basics, http://addictionrecoverybasics.com/ are-women-more-vulnerable-to-alcohols-effects/ (accessed September 2, 2011).

3. MedicOnWeb.com, "Alcohol Statistics," April 16, 2011, http:// mediconweb.com/health-wellness/alcohol-statistics/ (accessed September 2, 2011).

4. Ibid.

5. Ibid.

6. Ibid.

7. Ibid.

8. US Department of Health and Human Services, Office of Applied Studies, "The DAWN Report: Trends in Emergency Room Visits for Drug-Related Suicide Attempts Among Females: 2005 and 2009" and "The TEDS Report: Substance Abuse Treatment Admissions Aged 12 to 14," summaries available at "Substance Abuse and Mental Health Statistics," September 1, 2011, http://oas.samhsa.gov/ (accessed September 2, 2011).

9. US Department of Health and Human Services, Office of Applied Studies, "The DAWN Report: Emergency Department Visits Involving Underage Alcohol Use in Combination With Other Drugs," summary available at "Substance Abuse and Mental Health Statistics," September 1, 2011, http://oas.samhsa .gov/ (accessed September 2, 2011).

10. The Alcoholism Guide, "Alcohol Abuse Statistics," http:// www.the-alcoholism-guide.org/alcohol-abuse-statistics .html#axzz1TzEI5WVz (accessed September 2, 2011).

11. American Foundation for Suicide Prevention, "Facts and Figures: National Statistics," http://www.afsp.org/index.cfm?fuseaction =home.viewpage&page_id=050fea9f-b064-4092-b1135c3a 70de1fda (accessed September 2, 2011).

12. CollegeDrinkingPrevention.gov, "A Snapshot of Annual High-Risk College Drinking Consequences," July 1, 2010, http://www .collegedrinkingprevention.gov/statssummaries/snapshot.aspx (accessed September 2, 2011).

13. RAINN.org, "The Offenders," http://www.rainn.org/get -information/statistics/sexual-assault-offenders (accessed September 2, 2011).

14. The Alcoholism Guide, "Alcohol Abuse Statistics."

15. Stan E. DeKoven, *Family Violence: Patterns of Destruction* (n.p.: Vision Christian Ministries, 1999), 50.

16. For more information about John Eckhardt's spiritual warfare books, visit Charisma House's website at http://www .charismahouse.com.

17. Jessie Penn-Lewis, *Spiritual Warfare* (n.p.: Christian Literature Crusade, 1989), 41.

18. Ibid., 60.

CHAPTER 9
PROTECT YOUR HOME WITH A SECURITY SYSTEM

1. Lester Sumrall, *The Militant Church* (Tulsa, OK: Harrison House, 1990).

CHAPTER 10
THE HEALING POWER OF FRIENDSHIP AND INTIMACY

1. H. Norman Wright, *Making Your Love Last Forever* (New York: Inspirational Press, 1974), 358–359.

2. Romance Writers of America, "About the Romance Genre— Romance Literature Statistics: Readership Statistics," survey done in May 2009, http://www.rwa.org/cs/readership_stats (accessed September 2, 2011).

3. DeKoven, *Marriage and Family Life*, 92.

4. Mark Gungor, *Laugh Your Way to a Better Marriage* (New York: Atria Books, 2009), 74–75.

5. Gary Smalley and John Trent, *Love Is a Decision* (Dallas: Word Publishing, 1989), 59.

CONCLUSION
YOU CAN HAVE A SUPERNATURAL MARRIAGE

1. Hannah Hurnard, *Kingdom of Love* (Wheaton, IL: Tyndale House, 1978), 79–80.

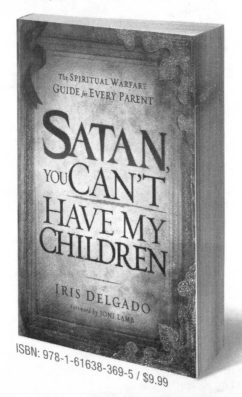